Stephanie,
Best luck in
the change process.

Harry Woodward

AFTERSHOCK

Helping People
Through
Corporate Change

AFTERSHOCK

Helping People
Through
Corporate Change

Harry Woodward
Steve Buchholz

Wilson Learning Corporation

Edited by
Kären Hess

John Wiley & Sons, Inc.
New York • Chichester • Brisbane • Toronto • Singapore

Publisher: Stephen Kippur
Editor: David Sobel
Managing Editor: Andrew Hoffer
Editing, Design & Production: Publications Development Company

Library of Congress Cataloging-in-Publication Data

Woodward, Harry
    Aftershock: helping people through
    corporate change.

    Bibliography: p. 224
    Includes index.
    1. Work groups. 2. Industrial organization.
I. Buchholz, Steve. II. Hess, Kären. III. Wilson
Learning Corporation. IV. Title.

ISBN 0-471-62478-0

Printed in the United States of America
  10 9 8 7 6 5 4

CONTRIBUTORS

Jane Agar	J. P. Morgan & Company
Betty Bates	Pacific Bell
John Enright	Consultant
Henry Griffiths	IBM-UK
Sue Lampson	Consultant
George Land	Consultant
Velma Lashbrook	Wilson Learning Corporation
S. Michael Moss	J. P. Morgan & Company
Bill Payne	Consultant
John Sullivan	Wilson Learning Corporation
Karon Wendt	Consultant

ACKNOWLEDGMENTS

Thank you to Donna Roberts, Cray Research, for her careful review of the manuscript and her assistance in obtaining permission to use "The Cray Style." Thank you also to Steve Cohen and Dick Leider for their thoughtful reading of the manuscript and their valuable comments and insights.

A corporate thank you goes to the sales force, product development personnel, and support staff of Wilson Learning Corporation for their contribution to the process of understanding change and its effects on people in organizations. A special thank you to Aleta Millette who skillfully and patiently coordinated development of the book. Finally, thank you to David Sobel, Andrew Hoffer, and Nancy Land for their expert guidance and suggestions during the production of AFTERSHOCK.

ACKNOWLEDGMENTS

CONTENTS

INTRODUCTION
From Future Shock
to Aftershock

AFTERSHOCK. What is it? Imagine a stylized drawing, an aerial view, of a community; picture the houses, schools, parks, a few lakes, churches, stores, a small river, and the offices of a mid-sized corporation. The drawing presents a pleasant scene, a stable, comfortable community.

Now the scene begins to change. Rumor has it that *something* is about to occur in the corporation, and ripples begin to radiate out from corporate headquarters. The rumors intensify and finally become real: reorganization, job redefinitions, layoffs. The ripples become more pronounced—they radiate out farther and farther and begin to touch other areas of the community. Soon new sets of ripples begin to radiate from houses, stores, schools, and churches. Before long the community is engulfed in a series of interlocking rings, looking like the transformed surface of a calm pond into which you have suddenly thrown a handful of pebbles.

This is a visual image of aftershock—a metaphor. Whether you live in a small community or a large city, the effects of change are like a web of ripples. One event affects another and, in turn, is affected by the reverberations that come back.

The process feeds off itself, continually intensifying and building. The effect on people is fear, anger, confusion, and a loss of control.

Even though people know a change is coming and even though they understand it intellectually, it still has an emotional impact that they don't quite expect and that they find difficult to cope with. The purpose of this book is to help people begin the coping process.

This process, moreover, is not intended to make change suddenly go away. The pond seldom returns quickly to its former calmness. Rather, the task of this process is to give people the tools to deal with the effects of what appears to be a steadily increasing rate of change.

CHANGE

Change is one of the foremost issues, if not *the* foremost business issue, of our day. Beginning roughly with the publication of Alvin Toffler's *Future Shock* in 1970, "Change"— with a capital "C"—entered the corporate lexicon as a word describing a mixed blessing. On the one hand, change represented growth, opportunity, and innovation; on the other hand, threat, disorientation, and upheaval.

Like it or not, change has become the norm. The relatively steady, predictable economic growth that characterized the post-World War II period has given way to rapid increases in competition, technical innovation, limited resources, and changes in attitude about work, male-female roles, and management.

More recent books such as *Megatrends*, *The Changemasters*, and *In Search of Excellence*, all underscore the fact that our culture in general and business in particular have come to accept the aphorism: "Change is the only constant."

Aftershock: Helping People Through Corporate Change is a response to a felt need on the part of organizations to understand and deal with change. Based on research, on painful experience, and on two successful Wilson Learning seminars developed to help managers and those with whom they work deal with change, the book is written for those who find themselves faced with change issues and feeling the pain. These issues may be reorganization, automation, rapid growth, downsizing, job redefinition, a physical move, the effects of competition, or a shifting market. Whatever the "trigger," people are experiencing confusion, worry, anger, numbness, or all of the above. The primary questions they are asking are, "What will happen?" "Will we get through this in one piece?" "Will it be smooth or will it be rough?" John Enright characterizes the situation with an analogy:

> . . . a branch floats peacefully down a river whose waters are high with the spring run-off. Although the branch is floating rapidly and occasionally bumps gently into a rock, it is almost effortlessly motionless in relation to the water it floats in. A similar branch has become wedged between some rocks, and is thus resisting the swift flow of water around it. This branch is buffeted, whipped, and battered by the water and debris floating past it, and will soon be broken by the pressure against it. If branches could experience, the one wedged into the rocks would be experiencing change with intense pain and distress; the floating one would experience ease and, paradoxically, comfortable stability even in the midst of rapid motion.

Expanding on Enright's analogy, people can experience change as being stuck or floating free; pain and dizzying motion or freedom and exhilaration. The key concept in all these experiences, however, is *movement,* or the lack of it. Likewise, this book has as its operative word . . . *movement.*

PURPOSE

The purpose of *Aftershock* is not to "prevent" or "solve" or "cure," but rather to help people *move* more freely through the change process. Specifically, the aims of the book are:

- To provide a set of strategies and skills people in change can use to manage the change process.

- To minimize the people "breakage" that often accompanies change, that is, to help reduce the pain and dislocation people feel during a change experience.

- To maximize the new opportunities that change presents for people and organizations.

FUTURE SHOCK and AFTERSHOCK

Toffler's *Future Shock* predicted a rapid increase in the rate of change and offered some general guidelines to prepare for and deal with its effects. His book and the majority of books and seminars on change since Toffler take a *strategic* approach; that is, they help you discern trends, plan for the future, and be, in effect, a "change engineer." They address the question, "How can I prepare for and anticipate change so that when it comes, I'll be ready for it?" *Aftershock,* in contrast, takes a *tactical* approach. It is not concerned so much with anticipating the future, as with dealing with the present. It answers the question, "Now that change has occurred, what do I do?"

Typically, when change occurs in organizations, people, particularly managers, tend to hurriedly plan, set objectives, gather information, and "sell" the change. They have to scramble and often find themselves buying into the change in principle, but feeling like victims because they suddenly have to implement it. They may feel two-faced having to promote a new plan they do not understand or fully agree with. As a result, people tend to focus on the technical issues only; that is, they jump headlong into the mechanics of planning, budgeting, or staffing and ignore their own and other people's feelings and attitudes. "We haven't got time for feelings," they say. "We're too busy."

In a change situation, however, people problems are much greater than technical problems. This is not to say that the technical problems are not important; they are. But if people are confused, angry, or have misgivings about the change—and their feelings and attitudes are not dealt with—the change will not proceed smoothly. *Aftershock* focuses on people problems, on maintaining high performance while minimizing people "breakage."

People "breakage" is the result of resistance—"hanging on." When people are either unwilling or unable to cope with the effects of change, they cling to the familiar or to the past. They lose their ability to see change for what it can become. They see change only in terms of what it is taking away. One way to understand this reaction is in the terms of Endings, Transitions, and Beginnings.

ENDINGS, TRANSITIONS, BEGINNINGS

When change occurs, something ends. Immediately then, people want something else to begin. They want something to suddenly fill the void that the ending created. Unfortunately, this magic solution seldom occurs. Thus, a transition is needed, a way to bridge the gap from the ending to the new beginning.

Although this progression makes sense logically, it is seldom implemented operationally. Instead, organizations tend to "jump to beginnings." Specifically, the culture of an organization in change tends to place its primary focus on the opportunities and promise of the new organization or plan and neglects the reactions of the employees. Indeed, people who express concern, worry, or even confusion about the new system are often told they have a "bad attitude."

Further complicating the change process is the fact that not everybody is at the same place at the same time. While some are at the ending stage, others are moving into transitions and beginnings. Also, people in organizations usually experience change less as a single event than as a series of change events. As a result, people in a changing organization are simultaneously in endings, transitions, and beginnings, with a number of different changes. The organization, however, unable to cope at an operational level with such complication, prefers to push forward monolithically. So the change process moves forward. On the surface, the beginning is fully underway. But underneath, the neglected transitions and unresolved endings fester.

Because of this tendency to jump to beginnings, *Aftershock* places its focus on endings and transitions. It will help you answer two key questions, (1) How is change affecting people? and (2) How can I help myself and others move toward beginnings? The first question will help you focus on identifying the basic reactions to change; the second, on developing strategies to meet the needs underlying the individual reactions.

In all, a successful beginning depends on a successful ending and transition. The value of this process is expressed no more succinctly than in the following dialogue from *Hope for the Flowers:*

> "How does one become a butterfly?"
> "You must want to fly so much that you are willing to give up being a caterpillar."
> "You mean to die?"
> "Yes and no. What looks like you will die but what's really you will still live. Life is changed, not taken away. Isn't that different from those who die without ever becoming butterflies?"

FINAL ISSUES

Many organizational changes involve the elimination of jobs. Whether they are called "layoffs," "downsizing," or "furloughs," the effect is the same. People lose jobs. Thus, in changing organizations you find three categories of people: those who will *not* lose their jobs, those who *may* lose their jobs, and those who *will* lose their jobs. *Aftershock* offers skills to deal with the first two categories of people. It does not deal with the third category.

In other words, if you want aid in downsizing, *Aftershock* is not the best tool. That process involves assisting people in such things as writing resumes and offering job counseling and placement services. Other books and even companies specialize in this area.

With those who are not laid off, however, *Aftershock* offers practical strategies and skills. It discusses not only the process of moving through change, but also addresses the sense of guilt sometimes felt by those who are not laid off—the "survivors." It also offers people who may *feel* that the change has rendered them incompetent or obsolete a method to recognize skills and develop connections, and thereby find a new, secure position in the organization.

Also, because of its focus on application—on strategies and skills—the format of *Aftershock* is at times unorthodox. In addition to the sentences and paragraphs of standard exposition, the book includes exercises, dialogue in script form, and case studies. Thus, while reading about managing in a changing environment, you, the reader, are asked to manage in a changing manuscript. The purpose of these various formats is to enable you to deal with change not only conceptually, but at certain points to also participate in the process by accessing actual experiences—your own and those of specific cases cited.

Change is seldom easy. And the hardest part of change is most often not technical, but attitudinal—letting go— recognizing what has ended and then moving on through transitions to beginnings. This process cannot be rushed, nor should it be dragged out. The key is striking a balance. The intent in this book is to offer the skills and knowledge that can help you strike the best balance for your own change situation.

1

CHANGE: THE ONLY CONSTANT

The world doesn't fear a new idea.
What it fears is a new experience.
D. H. Lawrence

Yes, *we're experiencing change. My*
people are coming to me—mad,
confused, worried, and some of them
I can't even read—and I don't know
what to do.
Manager in a change situation

When asked, "Are you experiencing change in your organization?" people seldom say, "No." Change is the norm, the only constant. Indeed, people in organizations often take pride in their ability to ride the waves of change and constantly adapt. They accept change as normal; they have become hardened to it.

People in organizations also generally agree that, "of late" (usually defined as the past ten to fifteen years), the *rate of change* has steadily increased, as has the amount of information with which people have to deal. For example, one issue of *The New York Times* contains as much information as a sixteenth-century person would have had to deal with during an entire lifetime.

In the early 1970s, Toffler and others gave a name to this phenomenon: *exponential growth*—the geometric doubling and redoubling of change given the rapid advances in our society. Toffler also predicted the results of change. Not surprisingly, he foresaw increased tension and disorientation. To combat these problems, Toffler offered some basic survival skills. We would, he said, have to learn *how to learn*, learn *how to relate*, and learn *how to decide*.

So we were warned and equipped. We accepted change as a continually accelerating process; we had a name to describe the process, and we had a set of generic skills to deal with it. To the question, "Are you experiencing change in your organization?" the answer was an automatic, "Yes." Indeed, if you were not experiencing change, something was probably wrong with your organization.

A DIFFERENT "YES"

Since *Future Shock*, the scenario Toffler laid out has generally come to pass, but with consequences and emotional costs nobody could have predicted. In 1984 John Enright observed:

Changes in life and work are coming faster and faster, with every indication that the pace of change will continue to increase. Change is rendering obsolete not only the equipment, tools, and technology in the organizations that managers manage, and the skills associated with that technology, but also the managing skills and attitudes which the manager so laboriously learned. With changes and this obsolescence come, for many, increasing pain and anxiety.

Enright's observation that change is "coming faster and faster" sounds like vintage Toffler. But his talk of the "pain and anxiety" of "laboriously learned" management skills becoming "obsolete" strikes a new chord—more immediate, more emotional.

Adding detail to the picture, Velma Lashbrook observes:

Globalization, protectionism, regional economic slumps, regulation, deregulation, takeovers, mergers, acquisitions, diversification, product liability, competition, product proliferation, downsizing, and declining profits—these are just a few of the factors affecting organizations. The scope and pace of change seems overwhelming.

She goes on to describe how in her

short six years in business I have experienced within my own organization the transition from entrepreneurial to professional management, the transition from a sales-driven to market-driven company, the internationalization of the business, our acquisition by a publishing company, our acquisition of an assessment company, the creation of two new divisions, product proliferation, increased customization of products and services, rapid growth, decreased profitability, layoffs, annual reorganizations . . . and I'm not alone. Most organizations with whom we consult have experienced equally significant changes. In most cases the complexity of change is magnified by the size of the organizations undergoing change.

Overall, the change from 1970 to the mid- and late-1980s can be put simply: the tone of the "yes" has changed. From a matter-of-fact, "Yes, of course we are experiencing change . . . isn't everybody?" we now hear a more strident, "Yes, we are experiencing change. My people are coming to me—mad, confused, worried, and some of them I can't even read—and I don't know *what* to do."

Specifically, the increase in the rate of change has made doing business less predictable; the increase in competition has called into question assumptions about marketing and production; and the shifting values of workers has called into question the use of traditional management techniques.

In the past three or four years, we at Wilson Learning have seen a groundswell of clients coming to us asking questions like, "Have you got a course on change?" or, "Do you have something in stress management?" Our response to their questions was initially, "Yes and no." We had elements dealing with change in the environment and change within business, but they were more strategic in their focus. The questions of our clients, however, seemed to be more tactical. They weren't looking for a course on predicting or preparing for change; they were looking for a course on dealing with the headaches. So, in response to these questions, we immediately began to develop interventions to help companies work through what appeared to be some pretty large disruptions.

After making it known that we were at work on a "change course," we talked with several companies about partnering with us in developing such a course. While it was still in its early developmental stages, we had requests for information and even for some purchases of a potential product, sight unseen. Then, in the midst of developing the change materials, we experienced a radical change in our own company. And we handled it poorly—so poorly, in fact, that a year later we had to repeat a similar process to rectify some of the mistakes we had made the first time.

From these experiences we learned two things: (1) no company is immune to substantial change, not even a company whose job it is to help other people through changes, and (2) change is no longer an "issue" simply to be discussed. Rather change has become a "painful experience"—one that has to be addressed immediately.

Enright suggests that change is experienced as painful because: "it is easier to see what is going than what is coming. . . . With the stepping-up of the pace of change, we must either prepare for ever-increasing pain, or change how we deal with change."

One interesting aspect of our and other organizations' sense of pain was its suddenness. "After all," one might ask, "didn't we see it coming? Hadn't Toffler and others predicted it?"

The answer to both questions is "Yes." But recognizing the onset of change is one thing; dealing with its effect is quite another. In short, many organizations do not recognize the need for change and consequently experience the "boiled frog phenomenon." This phenomenon rests on a classic biology experiment dealing with frogs in hot water. A frog placed into a pan of boiling water simply jumps out. But a frog dropped into cool water which is then gradually brought to a boil will not jump out and eventually boils to death. The gradually rising heat at first provides comfort but then saps energy. And just at the point when the frog needs its strength to jump, it has none.

According to Tichy and Ulrich (1984): "Many organizations that are insensitive to gradually changing organizational thresholds are likely to become 'boiled frogs': they act in ignorant bliss of environmental triggers and eventually are doomed to failure." In other words, they know the water is getting hotter, but have not really considered what they will do when and if it boils—and when it *does* boil, they do not know how to get out.

A CASE IN POINT

Until now you have been reading about change in conceptual terms such as exponential growth, people breakage, diversification, and boiling water. It will be helpful now to turn to a specific example of a company and of people in change—call it Averco Corporation. Even though this is a fictional name, the Averco scenario combines the events and outcomes of about a half dozen actual organizations which have recently gone through a sudden and disruptive period of change.

Situation

Although sales were up, the cost of doing business was resulting in minimal profit. The reasons were obvious—too many people in support positions contributing to high over-head, uncontrolled expenses, and two expansion groups fail-ing to bring products to market.

The senior management committee spent several sessions weighing the various options for restoring a positive profit picture. These sessions were often emotional and full of de-bate concerning fear that any "solution" might contradict the purpose and values the organization traditionally held.

More specifically, the company had grown and profited from its birth twenty years before. During that time, the com-pany had built a strong culture of committed employees. The question was asked, "How could something that strong and that successful go wrong—and so suddenly?" Some said, "It couldn't. This is just an anomaly. Let's just stick to our guns and things will work out." Others said, "No. The problem is that we *haven't* stuck to our guns. We started to get into areas we had no business being in. *That* was our mistake. Let's get back to basics." Still others said, "We went into new areas because we *had* to, we had no choice, and we're not through yet. We've got to roll with the times and the economy—and if that means we have to change *our* culture, so be it."

Because of the diversity of viewpoints, there was no clear consensus or plan. Rather, the committee tried, as one person put it, "to have their cake and eat it too." They attempted to deal with the very real issue of survival, but at the same time retain some of their basic values and practices.

The Decision

The final decision was reduced to four basic steps:

1. Cut expenses to the bone and cut next year's budget by as much as 50 percent.
2. Eliminate revenues going to soft areas and new ventures not promising short-term revenues.
3. Move to a variable versus fixed expense system by off-loading certain parts of manufacturing and certain serv-ices to other companies and freelance workers.

4. Downsize by 30 percent the divisions' employee numbers by early retirement, relocation, and job placement within off-loaded business units and as freelance consultants.

The last decision was by far the most difficult because traditional values supported a full-employment policy. To minimize the people breakage, a concerted effort was planned to place all employees who were victims of the decision into jobs that hopefully would be better than what they had. Indeed, the company made every effort to place all its people into positions that were similar, if not identical, to their present positions and, in addition, were better paying.

The rationale was admirable, but employees experienced the decisions emotionally as termination and job loss. Even though they were in many cases financially better off, employees felt as though they were separated from their "family." One employee commented, "All I ever heard around here was how people worked for more than just money, that what they really wanted was a sense of belonging to a whole and doing something they enjoyed. Now you're telling me forget all that fulfillment jazz—and, oh, by the way, here's more money." Another observed, "If you had given me a choice, I probably would have chosen to go freelance. What bothers me is that you didn't give me the choice. You didn't ask me."

Those who retained employment and a steady income outside the company were the lucky ones. But in other cases management's plan did not work, and people lost their jobs. These people were understandably bitter, "If you had just laid me off, I would have accepted that. I'd have doubled my efforts and found a job. But no. You promised me a net, a similar position outside the company. So where is it? Gone! It dried up, and now I'm worse off than if you had just plain fired me in the first place."

When news of these events became known, the fears of the remaining employees escalated. But even before these consequences became known, back at the point when management's decisions and strategies were being decided upon behind closed doors, the work unit culture was already acting upon rumor and wild speculation. Groups of employees could be seen discussing the forthcoming events throughout the building. Focus on job performance and productivity was flat. People were numb with worry, sitting at their desks staring at the walls. Erroneous rumors and speculations very quickly became reality in their minds, and they began to act as though decisions had already been formalized. Employees determined not to relocate were using their productive energy to look into other job opportunities. Others lived in limbo, not knowing what to do—certainly not working as usual.

Overall, the company was on hold. The energy that would normally have been used to be productive was shunted into nonproductive energy. Some people got angry. Others withdrew. Some walked around in a daze. And others thought the whole thing was great and voiced the opinion that this, "should have started a year ago."

The Change Trigger

Finally, upper management emerged from behind closed doors and announced their decision—to middle management. "*You* tell the employees," they said. "*You're* middle management. That's your job." After that, upper management personnel were suddenly unavailable—traveling, too busy to talk to anybody. Some even took vacations. The marching orders to middle management were:

- Cut expenses.
- Cut budgets.
- Reduce the number of employees.
- Stop all the rumors.
- Get remaining employees back on track producing and performing as fast as possible.
- Minimize people breakage.
- Restore morale.

These statements were communicated in varying degrees to different managers. Some got one story; some got another. Quickly they began to compare notes. "Cut expenses, cut budgets, reduce employee numbers are things I can understand," said one. "It won't be pleasant or easy, but at least I can implement them. But stop rumors? How do you stop a rumor? Or restore morale? Or get people performing and producing ASAP? Who are they kidding?"

Middle management's incredulity over the "orders" fell on sympathetic, but basically unresponsive ears. Upper management said, "We know it's going to be tough, and we don't have any better ideas on how to do it than you do. But be sure to let us know if we can help."

In reply to this sincere and well-intentioned offer, middle management said, "Thanks . . ." and turning away, mumbled ". . . for nothing." They had received verbal support, but little else. The central message still stood: Make things happen and make them happen fast.

Implementation

Most of the managers agreed that the decisions were justified, but emotionally they were not ready to be catalysts for change. The comment heard most often was like this one, made by the manager in the operations area, "I understand the decisions, and I guess I agree with them, but the way the whole thing was handled couldn't have been worse, and now *we* have the hot potato."

Managers saw two major obstacles.

1. *The Rumor Mill.*   Work units were operating on hearsay and rumor, reacting to every new tidbit of "news," and, in general, not trusting that they were getting accurate or true information from any area of management. They had been blindsided and told half-truths too many times.
2. *Their Skill Level.* Managers could cut budgets, expenses, and people, but basically felt a lack of skills in minimizing people breakage and restoring morale. "How do you do that?" one person protested. "Wave a wand?"

True, some managers welcomed the decisions because they understood the long-term purpose and moved quickly to mobilize for change. They felt they had something to gain. But in general, managers felt victimized for a variety of reasons:

1. Some felt angered because they were told, not asked. They felt they could have contributed to formulating a strategy if they had been asked for input. Consequently, they felt no ownership of the change and merely went through the motions of implementing it.

2. Some found the changes difficult because of their attachment to the way things were. These people often became angry and spread their discontent to others.

3. Others reacted out of a feeling of loss and used their energy to gain back or prevent as much loss as possible. Many of these people saw their job as "ministering" to other employees.

4. Some saw their roles as merely communicating the organization's wishes—a sense of transparency. They were frightened for the most part. They didn't want to be seen lest they become new targets. "Keep your head down," they said.

5. Others fought hard from the perspective of the employee, often communicating a sense of indignation at the injustices of the change process.

In all these cases, managers were having difficulty putting any energy into the job. Instead, they were using their energy to *react, resist,* and *defend*—not to manage the change environment.

Employee Reactions

Whether managers were positive, neutral, or negative toward the change event, they all faced a major challenge—how to align the remaining work unit on the new beginning. The business issues of expenses and budget were punishing, but the real issue was people. In general, people found themselves reacting in one or more of the following ways:

• Some were angry and either dumped on the manager, shared their discontent with other employees making them angry, or let it fester inside them, not risking venting their feelings.

- Some felt a lack of direction and spent energy wondering where things were going, not knowing what was expected, and fearing further changes. Often these people scurried about being "busy," but not really doing anything.
- Some were hanging on to what *was* and not accepting what was going to be. Given new job assignments, they simply continued doing their old jobs.
- Some quit mentally, but stayed physically, stepping out of the events, acquiescing to the manager's direction, but with little commitment.
- Certain people aligned themselves with other employees to form informal coalitions using time to play "ain't it awful."

IN SUMMARY

The culture of the organization seemed to change overnight. People left one company on Friday, and when they came to work the following Monday, it was a different company. Many of the technical skills that had been useful before were now seemingly outmoded or in question. All of the values people had come to accept now seemed transparent. All the energy that employees used to put into their work was now being diverted into dealing with emotions. And all the while they were straining to retain the appearance of serenity and efficiency for their customers.

Employees and managers were playing out in their minds all sorts of dire scenarios. Most of these negative projections never came to pass, of course, at least not to the extent that many had imagined, but at that moment it *felt* as though everything was going to happen. As one employee put it, "I think things will probably turn out okay, but right now it feels like the end of the world."

Six Months Later

Six months after the initial change, the company appeared to be coping, but with some interesting differences. For example:

- Some work units had restored high morale; others had low morale.

- In some areas people seemed to be adapting and working through the change. In others there was still bitterness and resistance.
- Some work units had made increases in productivity, while others were still down, in some cases by as much as 20 percent.

In short, some people and departments had a more rapid return to productivity and acceptance.

Some people and departments worked through most of the obstacles in about six months. Others, however, took longer. Even at nine or ten months, they still had relatively high levels of resistance and low levels of productivity.

What caused these differences? Circumstances? Perhaps. But in some areas where the basic circumstances were the same, there were significant differences in both productivity and attitude.

The more significant causes of these differences were the responses of individual managers, supervisors, and employees. Some had developed strategies, both organizational and personal, to shorten the time it took to recover.

What were these strategies—or more generally, what are some strategies that can be employed to help people and organizations through change? The remainder of this book will answer that question. You will be given an overview of the change process and be introduced to concepts and skills that you can apply to yourself and others in reducing the recovery period, thereby increasing the rate which you and the people who work with you move through the change process.

FRONT WHEEL VERSUS BACK WHEEL

As mentioned, much of the literature and courses about change deal with change from a "strategic" point of view, that is, as theories of change, trend analysis, or change engineering. This is the general's approach—moving pins around on a map. It involves strategic planning. But, as Enright suggests: "Qualitative, innovative change is not likely to come from careful planning, which can only incrementally extend what is already known. Left to their own devices," he continues, "caterpillars would generally produce fatter caterpillars—quantitative change—rather than butterflies—qualitative change!"

In contrast to the strategic approach, this book asks the tactical—"in the trenches"—question:

Now that a change has taken place, how do I deal with it?

Specifically, how can I help myself and the people who work with me understand and accept the change? What strategies and skills do I need to handle the change process and turn the pain into something positive?

One way to visualize this tactical, people-oriented approach is with a bicycle. The two wheels of a bicycle have different purposes. The back wheel powers the bike; the front wheel steers it. Extending this analogy to an organization, "back-wheel" skills are the technical and organizational skills needed for the organization to function. "Front-wheel" skills are the interpersonal "people management" skills. Corporations tend to rely on their back-wheel, that is, their technical skills.

People in corporations generally are recognized and promoted because of their back-wheel "expertise," not because of

their front-wheel people skills. This does not mean that they do not have people skills or cannot learn them—only that promotions are generally for back-wheel reasons. But today no organization can survive solely on its back-wheel skills. Like a powerfully driven bicycle with no one steering it, it will run into trouble very quickly.

Typically, however, when change comes, the response of organizations is primarily a back-wheel response—do what we know best. But the real need is for front-wheel skills, that is, helping people understand and adapt to the changing environment.

Consequently, in this book the focus is front-wheel. You know the back-wheel of your environment. We cannot presume to tell you what to do in that area. But, we can *offer* possibly helpful front-wheel skills, interpersonal techniques, and insights to reduce the pain of people's reactions to change and help them move through it more easily.

BASIC PREMISES REGARDING CHANGE

Four basic premises regarding change are at the core of the philosophy and approach suggested in this book.

1. *The change "trigger" is often beyond the control of the on-line people.* Most change decisions are made by senior-level management, often in response to larger cultural or economic forces. They are outside the average employee's control. For example, when top management decides to downsize, to lay off employees, the on-line managers, supervisors, and workers are rarely consulted.

2. *The central focus must be on the impact of change on people.* Although, as noted, most people tend to think of change as a marketing, strategic, or technical issue, the real issues around change are emotional. The most pressing issues surrounding change are the human issues. The core issue underlying resistance to switching from a typewriter to a word processor, for example, is likely to be related to recognition, self-esteem, or other personal factors, not to the technical factors of efficiency or keyboard configuration.

3. *People's actions, behavior, and communication are key to the successful implementation of change.* A manager's behavior during the change process becomes symbolic. If people view the manager as resisting the change, they will not be likely to embrace it themselves. For example, if a manager or supervisor does not attend the formal reorganization announcement, what does that say to the employees? The manager's positive acceptance of a change and its reflection on his or her behavior is key to implementing change.

4. *During change, the most effective way to proceed is to manage yourself first, and then influence others.* In change situations, you have to handle yourself personally before you can realistically expect to influence others. For example, if you do not know where you are going, how can you lead others? You may have seen the baseball cap with the two brims facing opposite directions and the saying, "I'm their leader—which way did they go?"

HOW DO YOU VIEW CHANGE?

Everyone looks at change differently. Some view it as positive and necessary; others view it as a problem. To help you identify more concretely with the concepts and skills presented in this book, please take a few minutes to reflect on how you view change. To begin, think of a change situation you are currently experiencing. A "change situation" is defined as any business, career-related, or personal experience requiring a significant change in your performance or attitude. Think

FIGURE 1   Based upon your description of this change situation, rate your feelings during this change using the scales below. For example, if your felt that the change was more of a Threat than an Opportunity, you would circle either a 2 or a 4 on the scale below. Please circle only one response for each pair of words.

1. Threat	0	2	4	6	8	10	Opportunity
2. Holding on to the past	0	2	4	6	8	10	Reaching for the future
3. Immobilized	0	2	4	6	8	10	Activated
4. Rigid	0	2	4	6	8	10	Versatile
5. A loss	0	2	4	6	8	10	A gain
6. Victim of change	0	2	4	6	8	10	Agent of change
7. Reactive	0	2	4	6	8	10	Proactive
8. Focused on the past	0	2	4	6	8	10	Focused on the future
9. Separate from change	0	2	4	6	8	10	Involved with change
10. Confused	0	2	4	6	8	10	Clear

about the events and the feelings you are experiencing during this change process:

1. What events immediately preceded the change?
2. How did you feel before the change?
3. What are your primary concerns about the change?
4. What are the consequences (real and potential) of the change to yourself and others?
5. How do you feel as a result of going through the change? (Have you noticed any attitude or behavior changes?)

As you progress through this book, keep in mind your beliefs about change and how you can work to make change a positive experience for you and those who work with you.

2

THE GROWTH CURVE: PHASES OF CHANGE

Grow or die.
George Land

*You hired me to run this department
and produce. You promoted me
because I was good at it. Now you want
me to improvise a new system? And on
top of that you want me to do a lot
of hand holding — listen to a lot of
bellyaching —and still keep up
production. You've gotta be nuts!*
Line manager in a changing company

Our discussion of change in general and the experience of Averco Corporation in particular raises two questions: (1) What happened? and (2) what do we do? Although these two questions are a matched set, people tend to gloss over the first and jump to the second. Particularly in a business setting, where the pressure is on to keep producing during disruptive change, the expectation is that people act quickly. The by-words of organizational life are "proactive," "action oriented," and "ready, fire, aim." This orientation *does* get results—but not always the best ones. Therefore, before learning about the strategies for dealing with change, step back and answer the first question:

What happened?

This question can be answered in two parts: What happened organizationally to Averco, and what happened and *is* happening to Averco's employees personally? To begin, consider the company in the larger context of growth. For that purpose you will use a model—the Growth Curve—which comes from general systems theory, specifically from the work of George Land. Land's model identifies general patterns of growth in a variety of "systems," ranging all the way from cellular and biological growth, to the stages of personal relationships, to the development of organizations. Land's findings are summed up succinctly in the title of his book, *Grow or Die*. He states that growth is natural and change inevitable. But at the point of major change, people tend to see the new beginning not as an opportunity, but as a threat. To try to stop the growth process, however, is to "die." So why do people do it?

Advertising suggests that people can "retain their youthful appearance." Some special interest groups feel the United

States should use embargos to help America return to the good old days when there wasn't any foreign competition. In some businesses there are movements to block an attempt to computerize operations systems because it is "dehumanizing." All these examples are denials of what is ultimately normal—natural growth. To begin, let's examine the larger question of growth and then focus on the relationship of growth to change.

THE GROWTH CURVE

The basic model (Figure 1) is represented by an "S" curve. Each of the three basic phases on the curve has specific attributes and outcomes.

The Formative Phase

When applied to an organization, Phase I, the formative phase, is the stage of the organization's coming into being, the time period in which it searches for an identity and a pattern. This phase generally is characterized by a strong sense of mission,

FIGURE 1   The Growth Curve/Phases of Change

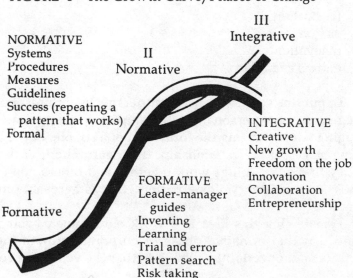

III
Integrative

NORMATIVE
Systems
Procedures
Measures
Guidelines
Success (repeating a
    pattern that works)
Formal

II
Normative

INTEGRATIVE
Creative
New growth
Freedom on the job
Innovation
Collaboration
Entrepreneurship

I
Formative

FORMATIVE
Leader-manager
    guides
Inventing
Learning
Trial and error
Pattern search
Risk taking

commitment, innovation, priority on marshaling resources, rapid growth, high market sensitivity, openness to ideas, willingness to take risks, unpredictability, activity, and high energy—getting the enterprise on its feet. This phase also includes a good deal of tension and uncertainty, as well as a longing for order and stability, a desire for increased structure.

In the formative phase, the task of the department/organization/individual is to invent or discover a viable pattern that works.

Key words that describe the formative phase are:

- excitement
- confusion
- inventing
- formation
- learning
- anxiety
- hope
- trial and error
- pattern search
- risk taking
- frustration
- elation
- innovation
- entrepreneurism

To put this stage in a different perspective, think about the beginning of a personal relationship. Two people meet and begin to date, starting the formation of a couple. In the beginning stages of the relationship, they learn about each other. They find some things work together and others don't. They look for consistency, for a pattern that is agreeable to both people.

Transferring this idea to a work environment, you would find that the formative phase of corporate growth includes tension and uncertainty about whether the venture is going to "make it," and correspondingly a longing for order and stability, a desire for increased structure and predictability.

Working in a Phase I company is a mixed experience. To some it is positive, exciting, and energizing; to others it is negative, worrisome, tense, and insecure. Other words to describe Phase I include chaotic, hectic, fun, confusing, promising, scary, hopeful, doubtful. In summary, the good news/bad news of the situation is that on the one hand you've got worry, anxiety, and confusion; on the other hand there is lots of energy and excitement, hope and promise, the sky's the limit— all driven by a very high level of energy.

At this stage *mistakes* are acceptable. Indeed, you probably would not even see them as mistakes at the time. Only in retrospect might you see a particular decision as a mistake. But in the midst of Phase I, when you do something that doesn't work, it's a learning opportunity. Compare it to a little child falling while learning to walk. Nobody looks at the fall as a mistake. It's simply a necessary part of learning.

Innovation in Phase I is not only valued, it is mandatory. You *have* to have innovation at this time because you do not have anything else. Ideas have substance and are highly valuable.

Market focus in Phase I is also very high. You're out there feeling the pulse of the customers. You want to know what they want, and you continually feed back that information.

Overall, the *goal* of this stage is to "make it," to succeed, to grow, to become predictable, to create stability, to eliminate all the "bad news" and realize all the "good news." In effect, the goal of Phase I is to get to Phase II.

The transition to Phase II is usually fairly smooth because it is incremental; it is done in a positive climate of growth, and it is seen as gain.

The Normative Phase

Phase II, the normative phase, is the stage of steady growth and the fine tuning of the system. The pattern for doing business has been developed and is working. This phase is characterized by stability, less energy and excitement, increased structure, and emphasis on efficiency.

**The normative phase is a period of high
productivity and profitability because the
successful pattern has been found and is
being replicated efficiently.**

The focus of this phase is on refinement, reinforcement, development, and elaboration of the pattern. Structuring becomes priority, and with increased structure comes increased hierarchy and a more direct management style. Less attention is paid to the marketplace.

Key words that describe the normative stage are:

- normal
- comfortable
- systematic
- boring
- procedured
- profitable
- structured
- guidelines
- repetition
- success
- replicating patterns
- formal

In the normative phase, the order and stability longed for in the first phase are finally achieved. In this state of "normalcy," the organization is running on its own, perfecting its systems, and usually building a pyramid of management.

Think back to the example about beginning a relationship. Now the couple has established a relationship, discovered a pattern of relating that is comfortable and secure, and continues to repeat that pattern. The two people settle in for a life together, set goals, make plans, and prepare for a long period of comfort and enjoyment.

In the same way, Phase II companies often assume that once they have made it, comfort and predictability are theirs. The high-tech industries, for example, during the time there was no competition from the Japanese, were in Phase II. The auto industry, during the long period in the 1950s and 1960s, cranked out automobiles, not paying much attention to the marketplace or any possible competition. Or AT&T, getting all their wires laid, enjoying their monopoly and Phase II success.

Like Phase I, working in a Phase II company can be a mixed experience. For some it is positive, predictable, comfortable, and profitable. It provides a sense of accomplishment and success. For others it is negative, boring, political, regimented, and business-as-usual. Roles are being decided, and the hierarchy begins to build. There are more standard operating procedures. No free-floating anymore.

Again, it is a good news/bad news situation. The good news is in the profit and the comfort; the bad news is that work is not quite as much fun; it is boring to some people. People who are deeply into formative, entrepreneurial activities do not like it anymore. The groove has become a rut, and they may leave at this point.

In Phase II, *mistakes* are definitely frowned upon. No longer viewed as "learning opportunities," they are regarded simply as mistakes, and you get your knuckles whacked if you make one. In this phase, mistakes "shouldn't" happen. One way to avoid mistakes is to avoid risk. People spend time doing things that are "safe."

Innovation is given lip-service approval, but is tacitly punished. Nobody is going to say he or she does not want innovation, but what they *do* say is, "Yes, you can innovate, *but* be sure your work is on time or within budget, or it doesn't take anything away from anything else." This response is antithetical to innovation. The organization, in effect, talks out of both sides of its mouth. Nobody wants to get rid of innovation because that is what got them to Phase II. So, basically, innovation is set on a pedestal in this stage, honored but not really practiced.

Alternatively, innovation becomes relegated to a particular department, like R&D. *They* can innovate. The budget may even designate funds for that department to innovate, but everyone else is supposed to make the system run, not innovate.

The *market focus* of Phase II companies is no longer high. More likely it is medium. Since you have developed this wonderful system, your focus is probably on *it*. So you do not pay as much attention to your market. If the market changes, you

probably don't want to know about it because that means that
this thing you have built has to be changed, and you don't
want to do that. So you pretend that nothing has changed.

The *goal* of Phase II is to stay there—forever—enjoying
steady growth with only incremental change.

This phase may last for a short time or a very long time, but
eventually things begin to change.

For a perspective on this change, think again of the relationship of two people. The pair has married, and the marriage
has become routine. It is predictable—and that is the trouble.
It is potentially unable to cope with external changes. The
media is full of stories focusing on these junctures in people's
lives. The woman, whose kids are self-sufficient, wants to go
back to school, but her husband cannot understand why she
wants to change. Or the man, who for personal reasons wants
to change careers, has a wife who cannot understand why he
wants to leave everything he has worked so hard for.

In corporations, this phase, late Phase II, is characterized
by a flattening out of the productive cycle. Tried and true
measures and procedures no longer work as well because of
outside forces such as competition, waning product life, market changes, or increasing costs.

The Averco Corporation experienced just such forces. The
company had begun 20 years earlier as a ten-person, one-
product company. Stories of the early days were still fresh in
everyone's memory. Phase I stories of how they took a chance
on a maverick product and made it work, how they sweated
out making ends meet those first years and almost did not
make payroll commitments. How their risks paid off, and how
valuable a simple idea was then. Characteristic of these stories—like most remembrances of the formative phase—was
the tendency to remember the excitement and forget, or at
least joke about, the tension. Finally, however, they established their own market niche.

In their Phase II heyday, they owned certain segments of the
market, and the product that owned that market was the original—the one on which the company was founded. Gradually,
however, the demand for that product diminished, while the
competition that had, for years, been eating away at their dom-
inance increased. This process had not gone unnoticed by

Averco—and they *had* developed new lines. But they were still wed both economically and sentimentally to their "bread and butter" product. So they continued to put off dealing directly with this erosion. That is, until some rapid market changes and increases in their own costs and overhead forced them to face the reality of what was going on.

In response to this realization, Averco did what many companies do at this juncture. The classic late Phase II responses are back-to-the-basics, do nothing, or redefinition.

Back-to-the-Basics

Companies resolve to work smarter, not harder. They reorganize, cut costs, and downsize—all for the purpose of extending Phase II. Interestingly, companies at this point see change as loss. Their model is "hanging in there." Underlying their actions is a fundamental inability to admit that the system is no longer working. Rather, they believe that the system is good, but has been weakened or compromised by neglect or by infatuation with new ideas. Ideally they want to cause the flattened Growth Curve to take an upswing as illustrated in Figure 2.

FIGURE 2   Back-to-the-Basics Growth Curve

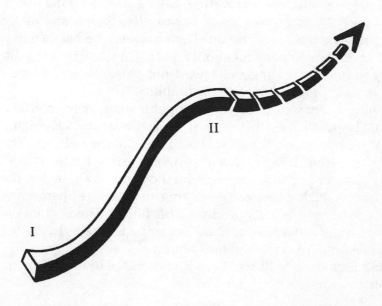

FIGURE 3   Do Nothing Growth Curve

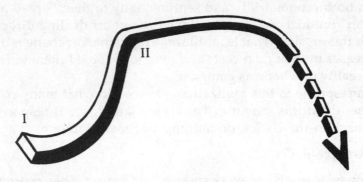

Do Nothing

Some companies refuse to admit that the water is heating up, making themselves candidates for boiled frogs. In response to their inaction, the curve not only stays flat, but actually takes a downturn, as illustrated in Figure 3. Thus, their model for change becomes crisis.

Redefinition

In anticipation of the late Phase II flattening, companies return to some of the basic activities of Phase I—asking "what?" defining the business, innovating, taking risks, and the like.

Initially, Averco did a lot of back-to-the-basics, and doing nothing, and little redefinition. Their back-to-the-basics bump sustained the company for about a year. They reversed the dip they were experiencing and saw, if not a rise, at least a leveling in their productivity and profitability.

Things went well for a while. Upper management, in effect, said, "There. We're stable. Now if we just wait and keep doing what we know best, things will pick up." But they did not. The company went into another dip, which turned into a slide. This time upper management did nothing, waiting for the upturn—which never came—trying to convince themselves that the water was getting only a *little* hotter. Then, when the reality of the situation could no longer be ignored, they acted out of a sense of crisis and took action.

In summary, late Phase II can be described in the following terms:

- loss of market share
- attempts to facelift
- coalitions formation
- blaming
- panic
- back to basics
- denial

Unfortunately, the model for many organizations in change is, in terms of the Growth Curve, late Phase II in crisis. It has become axiomatic to many that change is synonymous with upheaval and pain. This need not be the case, however. Change can also be synonymous with renewal and satisfaction.

Although Averco experienced a good deal of pain, it could have been worse. At the point they decided to take their major action, they were still a profitable and effective organization. Their situation wasn't as dire as it may have seemed at the time. Still, they *did* have some very serious issues that needed to be faced. Whatever the balance, the action they took launched them into Phase III, the integrative phase.

The Integrative Phase

Phase III is the point at which redefinition occurs and the company takes a new direction. The late Phase II activities such as back-to-the-basics may look like redefinition, but they are reductive rather than expansive.

True Phase III activity is activity for the right reasons—to redefine, cast off outmoded models, innovate, and take risks. It is, as mentioned, a redisplaying of many of the activities associated with Phase I. But unlike Phase I, which starts afresh, Phase III is growing out of an existing and often very entrenched culture. All the operational and managerial models are tried and true Phase II models. Thus the transition from Phase II to Phase III is not without its hitches. Some of the major areas are described in the following paragraphs.

False Starts

Like Phase I, the success of Phase III is built on taking risks and trying things out. As a result, many of the new ideas, procedures, policies, organizations, and strategies do not work. The long-term result is a better organization. The short-term result is frustration and a sense (based on a Phase II mentality) that people should not be "making mistakes."

Chronic Uncertainty

Since things are basically up for grabs, employees have to develop a high tolerance for ambiguity and uncertainty. Also, coming out of a phase when most things were basically known and it was possible to give and take orders, it is often disorienting to be thrust into an environment where there are seemingly no rules and people are expected to take initiative.

"Organ Rejection"

Just as the human body will reject a transplanted organ, even though the body's life depends on it, organizations by their nature often work to kill the new system. Operationally, the old systems, although they are dying, are still in many ways stronger than the new systems. Thus by their strength alone they represent stability and workability in comparison to the new and emerging systems.

Interpersonally, many people will still cling to an "if it ain't broke, don't fix it" mentality. They demand of people who champion the new system a level of expertise and competence which these people cannot provide because they are still in a learning and experimentation phase.

Transition as an Event

The transition from Phase I to II is usually, as mentioned, an incremental process, controlled from the inside, and perceived as gain. Transition from Phase II to III, however, is just the opposite, a change spurred by exterior forces, seen as loss, and often perceived as sudden. In reality, however, the factors causing the change have probably been working for some period of time. Indeed, the actual economic forces, rising competition, increased costs, and market shifts that triggered the change may have been quite gradual in coming. But because of the tendency to downplay such forces, to ignore rumors, and to stick corporate collective heads in the Phase II sands; and because the heating up of these forces, like the frog's water, is so gradual, people do not perceive that there *is* a problem until an event makes them aware of it. This event may be a sudden rise in costs, a court ruling, legislation, or a reorganization announcement by upper management.

Whatever the trigger, two things are true: (1) People do not believe it until it happens, and (2) people mark time from "that day"—the point in time when the rumor they had been struggling with, hoping would go away, or denying, finally became a reality.

Mission Focused

Because part of the organization is starting anew, the traditional Phase II skill of breaking things into parts and dealing with them separately does not work anymore. Nobody knows what the new parts are, let alone how they fit together. It, therefore, becomes the company's job to simplify—to set a vision or mission before managers and employees and allow them to define the parts and put them together. Thus management marshals a series of known elements and people to accomplish a task, making management a less useful skill than leadership—providing a picture of the future and motivating people to work out the details.

Overnight Job Shifts

Because change is experienced as an event rather than a process, people's jobs can change literally overnight.

Operationally, new procedures and practices can be mandated very quickly, turning seasoned veterans into apprentice learners, turning competent employees into temporarily "incompetent" employees.

At a managerial level, the transition from Phase II to Phase III can be very trying. In Phase II the manager's job is to keep the corporate machine going. People are hired and reinforced for keeping the company moving along the lines it is supposed to be going. Managers rely on technical skills to keep the company producing. Employees are promoted because of their technical expertise. In fact, about 80 percent of what managers do is technical in nature, and 20 percent or less because the heating up of these forces, like the frog's water, is so gradual, people do not perceive that there *is* a problem until an event makes them aware of it. This event may be a sudden rise in costs, a court ruling, legislation, or a reorganization announcement by upper management.

Whatever the trigger, two things are true: (1) People do not believe it until it happens, and (2) people mark time from "that day"—the point in time when the rumor they had been struggling with, hoping would go away, or denying, finally became a reality.

Mission Focused

Because part of the organization is starting anew, the traditional Phase II skill of breaking things into parts and dealing with them separately does not work anymore. Nobody knows what the new parts are, let alone how they fit together. It, therefore, becomes the company's job to simplify—to set a vision or mission before managers and employees and allow them to define the parts and put them together. Thus management marshals a series of known elements and people to accomplish a task, making management a less useful skill than leadership—providing a picture of the future and motivating people to work out the details.

Overnight Job Shifts

Because change is experienced as an event rather than a process, people's jobs can change literally overnight.

Operationally, new procedures and practices can be mandated very quickly, turning seasoned veterans into apprentice learners, turning competent employees into temporarily "incompetent" employees.

At a managerial level, the transition from Phase II to Phase III can be very trying. In Phase II the manager's job is to keep the corporate machine going. People are hired and reinforced for keeping the company moving along the lines it is supposed to be going. Managers rely on technical skills to keep the company producing. Employees are promoted because of their technical expertise. In fact, about 80 percent of what managers do is technical in nature, and 20 percent or less

FIGURE 4   The transition from Phase II to Phase III

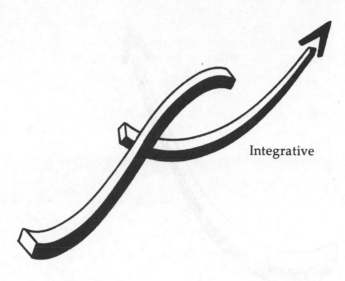

Integrative

IN SUMMARY

Ideally, companies would like the Growth Curve model to look like the one shown in Figure 5. In this ideal scenario, companies would move through the formative phase, into the normative phase, and continue indefinitely, that is, experience stability and growth forever.

But when change occurs and the curve begins to flatten out (Figure 6), it may look as if the company is going to lose effectiveness and eventually cease to exist. Actually, however, the company is just experiencing a normal pattern of change. It only *seems* like the end.

AT&T is a good example of a company that has just experienced this change. The directive in 1984 forced them to move rather abruptly from Phase II to Phase III. In some ways, AT&T had encouraged the divestiture. Federal regulations prevented the company from doing many of the things it had to do to survive. But it was still unprepared in many ways for the impact that the changes would have on its people. Changing from a service orientation to a marketing orientation was a major shift. The long-term challenge for AT&T is to maintain its newly rediscovered entrepreneurial spirit without losing its

FIGURE 5   Ideal Growth Curve

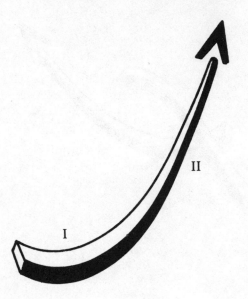

people and all that it has learned from being in business as long as it has been.

The best means to deal with the uncomfortable period of moving from Phase II to Phase III is to begin as early as possible

FIGURE 6   Normal Growth Curve up to Perceived (Broken Line)

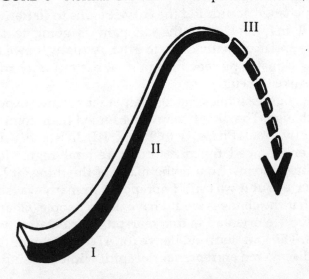

to prepare for change and begin to push out new procedures, markets, and the like *before* the company is too far into late Phase II survival behavior. The more you have happening, the better. See Figure 7.

Ideally, while the old system is being phased out, the new system is already underway. Even with this method, there are still bumps and problems, but not the total upheaval experienced when companies wait too long to implement change.

One final point to remember is that the Growth Curve is a very simplified model of a very complex phenomenon. Growth usually entails not just *one* change, but many changes. Most people in organizations experience change as an on-going series of events. A truer representation of this process is shown in Figure 8.

Instead of one large "S" curve, change is typically experienced as a whole series of little "s" curves. You may be at the formative phase of one, the normative of another, and the integrative of a third. Still, there are overall patterns as well, and despite the variations in the smaller changes, companies and people can often place themselves, in general, at either the formative, normative, or integrative stage.

FIGURE 7   Integration occurs

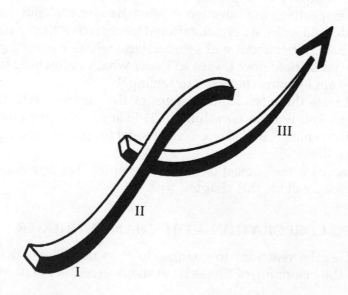

FIGURE 8   The Growth Curve Cycle

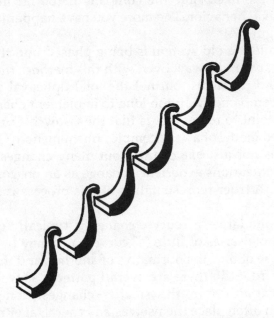

The Growth Curve is general, not specific. It does a better job of describing where a company is and how it got there than it does at predicting the future in any detail. In short, it provides contours to help people answer, from an organizational perspective, the question, "What happened?" But no sooner do you gain an organizational perspective than you need to ask, "What about me? I understand what's happening in the organization; now I want to know what's happening to me. Why am I feeling the way I'm feeling?"

To address these issues, the issues of the personal effects of change, you will do two things: (1) Examine the personal reactions to change, and (2) look at a model for understanding these reactions.

The model is the subject of the next chapter. The reactions themselves conclude this chapter.

AVERCO CORPORATION—THE CHANGE TRIGGER

To look at the reactions to change, look at the trigger that marked the beginning of Phase III at the Averco Corporation.

The final paragraph of their Marketing Strategy Report, dated March 15, ran as follows:

> In summary, we conclude that the market has shifted to a significant extent and we should seriously consider adjusting our marketing emphasis in Level One and Level Four products. Specifically, we recommend that Level One products will be phased out and Level Four products will be substantially improved and increased.

It sounded simple, but the impact on the organization would be profound. Level One comprised the company's original products—the products on which the company's history and identity rested. Level Four products were the most recent, and in some cases still untested, products. To make such a shift represented not only a gamble with the market, but also meant a large scale process of moving and retraining the Level One managers and employees in the new products and procedures of Level Four.

In response to the decision, the vice-president in charge of planning and development, Carter Moritz, issued the following memo to all Averco managers:

Memo

TO: Rick Everett, Elizabeth Lewis, John James,
              Ellen Anders, Dick Yates

FROM: Carter Moritz

DATE: April 3

RE: STRATEGIC PLANNING

I know most of you are curious about our next move in this undertaking. Please plan to attend an overview meeting on Monday the 7th.

The meeting took place on Monday, as scheduled. Carter explained the changes that were going to be implemented. He concluded with, "And, given the shift in the market, it's clear that Level One products simply aren't going to produce for us in the future the way they have in the past."

Several of the managers expressed shock and concern about the proposed change. John James stated, "To me it's a problem of balancing the two. Phasing in one level and phasing out the other with the minimum of disruption for our people. And I tell you, that's not going to be easy."

Carter acknowledged the difficulties facing the managers, "I realize this isn't going to be easy. A lot of people are going to be upset. And I know for some of you this is all pretty sudden. But putting the plan together hasn't been easy for us either. We had to move fast. And maybe we didn't always keep everybody in the loop, but there didn't seem to be much of a choice. Now it's up to you to implement the change. Let's get to it."

After the meeting, Rick Everett asked Carter how long he had known about the changes. When Carter acknowledged having known about them for several weeks, Rick asked— actually demanded—that they talk. Carter agreed, and the following conversation took place:

CARTER: Rick, believe me, I know how you feel. I'd feel the same way if I were in your place.

RICK: Can I ask you something right off the bat? Are we laying people off?

CARTER: Yes. I'm afraid we'll have to.

RICK: Who?

CARTER: We don't know that for sure. Probably no one in your area, but I can't be sure.

RICK: What about me?

CARTER: Relax. You won't be laid off. You're much too valuable to the company.

RICK: Well, okay, but how is this going to affect my area short term?

CARTER: There'll be changes. We're going to have to start phasing out Level One as soon as possible and integrating what we want to retain with certain Level Four products.

RICK: So you're talking about combining levels. Can you tell me—how are we going to do that? Does this mean that I'll have to share a job with John?

CARTER: Ahhh, perhaps. I think you and he will share some responsibilities, especially in Research and Design. That's critical.

RICK: Listen. What am I going to tell my people? You know the rumors are rampant around here. I've got people walking around in the halls wondering whether or not to buy another week's worth of meal tickets for the lunch room.

CARTER: Yeah, it's rough. I know. We may be able to distribute most of the jobs, but how we do that depends . . . .

RICK: Will you let me know the specifics of this as soon as possible?

CARTER: Yes. If I can.

RICK: I mean, I'm a little irritated that I wasn't let in on this from the very beginning.

CARTER: I understand how you feel. It's a big change. Times are changing, and we've gotta roll with this. We're losing our market share. We've been a creative and innovative company, and you've been one of the best. I want you to know that.

RICK: Um hum. Look, Carter, is there a time frame for any of this?

CARTER: Yes. We have to have this all in place by the beginning of the fiscal year.

RICK: You're talking a time frame of six weeks??!!

CARTER: We're talking six weeks.

RICK: Well, I don't know how we're going to do it.

Rick left the meeting room shaking his head, returned to his office, and dictated the following memo:

Memo

TO: Warren, Judy, Paul, Dennis, Peggy
FROM: Rick
DATE: April 7
RE: NEXT STEPS

There has been a lot of talk recently, and I realize you've been trying to get answers to your questions, with limited success. As a result of the Executive Committee meeting today, I think I can finally give you some more definitive answers. Let's get together tomorrow (the 8th) at 9:00 a.m.

When Warren received the memo, he angrily scrawled the following note to a co-worker: "Judy, I don't want to say I told you so, but . . . I told you so. They finally did it to us. See you at the meeting. We can all hear the verdict together."

The next day the members of Rick's team met and the following scenario occurred:

RICK: First, I want to assure you there probably won't be any layoffs in our division—only reassignments. But I can't guarantee that. Basically though, all of you—all of *us*—will have to start doing things we either haven't done or will have to learn. Level One products are being phased out and combined with Level Four. Now that's a big change. And, we have a six-week time frame to implement this new program. I'm as surprised about this as you are. I just found out about it yesterday, but I know we have a good team here, and I'm fully confident in all of you that you'll rise to the occasion to the best of your abilities.

Rick pauses to get reactions. There are none.

RICK: So, I'd like to get some feedback about how you feel about all this. I know it's kind of a shock, and it's new, but we really need to keep communicating here.

JUDY: Well, I've got a lot of questions.

An uncomfortably long pause follows, which Rick finally breaks.

RICK: Frankly, so do I. I know it's a big shakeup, but we really need to work as a team here. Peggy? Do you have any . . .

PEGGY: I think it's super! It's exactly where the company needs to be headed now—sort of reaching out. It's just very fast—six weeks—that's quick. But I think it's just great.

Warren glares at her, shaking his head in disbelief.

RICK: Warren? I can feel your tension from here. I wish you'd talk about how you feel about this.

WARREN: Tension? Whatever gave you that idea? Me? No! I have nothing to say.

RICK: Paul?

PAUL: (Obviously upset and self-absorbed, pauses and then comments unconvincingly) Fine. Let's see what happens.

DENNIS: I think in the face of everything, we've just got to stay positive.

RICK: Come on folks, talk to me.

Warren looks as though he will comment, then shakes his head.

RICK: Warren?

WARREN: No. I've got work to do.

Warren stalks angrily out of the room and the meeting breaks up.

WHAT'S WRONG WITH THIS PICTURE?

Carter Moritz answering Rick's concerns by telling him that "we've been a creative and innovative company, and you've been one of the best"—Rick trying, unsuccessfully, to promote the change with his people—Warren walking out on the meeting—all these images are indicators that Averco is due for a rough transition.

Technically, the reasons are clear. Averco prolonged late Phase II a little longer than they should have and, as a result, their transition from the normative to the integrative phase of their growth is going to be seen, initially at least, more as a crisis than as an opportunity.

In response to these events, both Carter and Rick do the same things: Write memos and call meetings. Neither person was particularly successful. People have left both meetings angry and confused. Their plan from here on in? Pass along information as it becomes available, plan, budget, and implement. In short, cope.

In Carter and Rick you see people falling back on what they know best, traditional management skills, when those skills are really no longer appropriate. This is not to say that they should not plan, budget, and implement. These tasks are necessary. But of greater importance now are other tasks— the tasks of Phase III managers: Self-management, leadership, defining a vision, and dealing with employee reactions. Without these, traditional management activities do little to help and sometimes actually hinder the change process.

Likewise, the employees, many of whom are taking a victim stance—"They did it to us"—are only making the situation worse.

WHAT NEEDS TO BE DONE?

Often times in change such as this one, the "vanilla" approach syndrome sets in. People decide that "if only we had _____, then everything would be Okay" or "if they would just do _____, then I wouldn't feel this way." A common example of a vanilla approach is information. "If we just had more information, then we could deal with this thing." But what if

Rick adopted this approach? Would more information solve his and his people's problems? In other words, who at that meeting might have felt better as a result of more information?

Judy might have; she was the one who said she had some questions. And Peggy as well, but she was already positive about the change. But Warren? Probably not. He's already got enough information to make him angry. More information might make him angrier. And Paul? There appears to be in him a concern that goes deeper than just lack of information. He is a little hard to read. Then take Dennis. He called for them all to "stay positive"—a request which under the circumstances would have been humorous if it had not been so inappropriate. And what about Rick? He could certainly use more information, but he is going to have to be more than just informed to manage the change. Right now he is a house divided, trying to advocate a change that he obviously doesn't believe in or accept himself. As a result, his meeting probably made the problem worse, not better.

At this point it would be easy to point out what Rick did wrong and what his people "should" do to deal with the change. But to do that would be to fall into the trap so many people in charge fall into—the trap of instant action, being "proactive" or, as mentioned earlier, "ready, fire, aim."

Different people need different things.

What is necessary first is not a specific action or vanilla approach. What *is* necessary is a strategy which takes into account both the technical and people issues—and begins with the people issues. As you saw, different people react differently to the same situation. Thus any single approach will reach only a small percentage of any group. So to begin, Rick and his people need to come to terms both with what they are feeling and what their specific needs are during this period. And one way to begin that process is to understand the impact of change on individuals, the focus of the next chapter.

3

THE CHANGE MODEL: ENDINGS, TRANSITIONS, BEGINNINGS

"Get on board," they tell me. "This new system is good for you. Try it; you'll like it." That's easy for them to say. They know what's going on. But before I can get behind this thing, I need some time to figure out what's going on and how I'm going to deal with having half of my job eliminated.

Employee going through change

THE "NEVER END" SCENARIO

There are as many changes as there are people. But there are also many similarities in different people's experience of change. Therefore, to begin this chapter, you will depart from the narrative and participate in a short exercise. Rather than simply reading about personal change, you will go through an exercise that will enable you to recall the events and recreate the feelings of an actual change in your life. The process is simple. All you have to do is recall an event and then answer five questions. If you take a few minutes to conscientiously complete this exercise, you will gain a deeper insight into the concepts you are reading about in this book.

- First, recall an experience that you didn't want to end—but *DID end.*

You obviously want to select something that was very good. You hoped it could go on forever. It could have been a job you once had or a relationship. (One person, in response to this first part of the exercise, wrote only three words: "Mary Jane Murphey.") It could have been in high school or college, any experience you had that you really liked. (Another person selected her summer as a volunteer firefighter.) It does not have to be business related. Go with the first thing that comes to mind. You never wanted it to end—but it did.

Now answer these questions:

1. **Before it ended, or before you knew it was going to end—in what is called the** *Golden Age* **of the experience—What was it like?** Obviously it was positive, so record your general feelings. But also think of it in terms of how you felt about your own *abilities.* And what were

your *relationships* with other people like during this time?

_____

_____

_____

2. **What caused it to end?** What were the events? Did you choose it? Or did it just happen? Why did it happen?

_____

_____

3. **When it ended, what was your initial response?** When the ending first hit you, your initial response was probably fairly strong. What was it? Try to sum it up in four or five words.

_____

_____

_____

4. **What was your secondary response?** After a certain amount of time—minutes, days, even a year—your initial response was replaced by a secondary, different response. What was it?

_____

_____

_____

5. **How did it turn out?** After everything was said and done and the dust settled, however long it took, was it a good thing? A bad thing? A little of both?

_____

_____

_____

What you have just done is *mapped* a change experience in your life. The details will be different for each person. But the basic reactions and feelings will be similar. To examine that, focus on Questions 1, 3, and 4.

Responses to Question 1, the Golden Age experiences, tend to run as follows: I felt good, happy, comfortable, content, stable, trusted, supported, secure, joyful. People at this stage know what to expect. Life is predictable. Terms to describe abilities include: felt competent, confident, recognized, valued. In this period, relationships with other people are typically easy, seem to flow, do not require a lot of time to develop, seem to happen naturally. Feelings are not held back, and there is a free flow of information. People get back as much as or more than they give.

Now move to Question 3, your initial reaction when the Golden Age is shattered. The most common responses are anger, fear, frustration, confusion, denial, panic, surprise, disbelief, and numbness. People may react by engaging in disruptive behavior, withdrawing, becoming disoriented, or grudgingly accepting.

Whereas answers to Questions 1 and 3 are fairly uniform, answers to Question 4, the secondary response, are diverse. Some respond neutrally. They say, "I've accepted it. I didn't necessarily like it, but I decided to move on; I started to generate some ideas; I started to look for alternatives; I started to look for help."

Other responses are positive, "I got excited; I really thought it was great; once I got over the shock, I saw all sorts of opportunities; I'm glad it happened; it was the best thing that ever happened to me."

A third group records negative feelings, "anger, fear, and panic." In other words, the secondary response continues the primary response either in an overt form or in muted feelings such as bitterness, sadness, loneliness, longing, nostalgia, or a sense of betrayal.

In answering this question, some groups are skewed to the negative, some to the positive, and some are split. This is interesting for two reasons:

1. Whereas the Golden Age feelings and the initial reactions to an ending are similar—everybody responds basically the same—secondary reactions tend to vary from person to person and from case to case. For example, you may have a positive secondary response in one situation and a neutral or negative one in another.

2. The common wisdom around secondary responses is that they are "supposed" to be basically positive or, at worst,

neutral. Most people have been admonished since child-hood to "buck up," "not cry over spilt milk," "get on with it," or be "proactive." If you feel other than neutral or posi-tive, you are likely to be told, "Don't feel that way." But the way you feel *is* the way you feel, regardless of what you're "supposed" to feel.

In summary, the positive feelings of the Golden Age and the pain of the initial reactions are *givens* in most change situa-tions. But the secondary reaction is open and, therefore, par-tially under your control.

To represent this process visually, imagine you had a pain chart. The Golden Age and the initial reaction would look like Figure 1. At the point of the ending, the pain rises abruptly. Before charting the secondary reaction, look at your response to Question 5, "How did it turn out?" Most people put down "okay" or "good" for this question. This isn't to say that all changes turn out well or that there aren't some lingering re-grets or disappointments, but on the average, most changes are perceived as neutral to positive overall. The eventual out-come can be represented graphically by adding one more point to the scale as in Figure 2.

Now the key question becomes, *"What does the line look like that connects the initial reaction and the eventual outcome?"* Since this line represents the secondary reaction, or the *transi-tion,* it will vary from person to person. One possibility is illus-trated in Figure 3.

FIGURE 1   Initial Reaction to an Ending

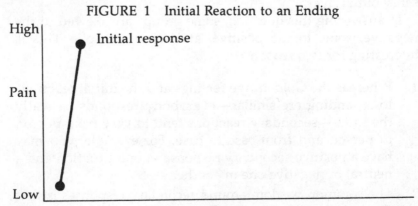

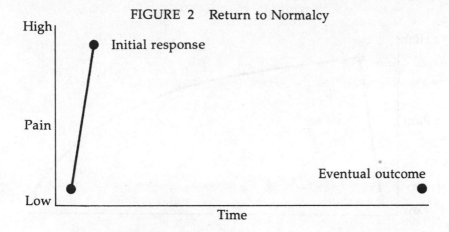

FIGURE 2   Return to Normalcy

This transition is possible, but not likely. People tend not to drop down that quickly. The pain of an ending takes time to work through. In fact, when people appear to recover from an ending quickly, there is a tendency to think they are fooling themselves and that sooner or later the reality of the situation might hit them and cause the chart to spike up.

Another possibility is illustrated in Figure 4. Again, this transition is possible, but not probable, although it is not uncommon for people to keep the pain of an ending at an artificially high level over time by their refusal to let go of hard feelings, anger, or frustration.

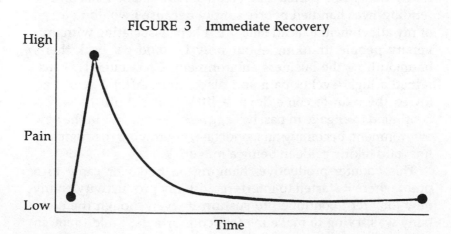

FIGURE 3   Immediate Recovery

FIGURE 4   Delayed Recovery

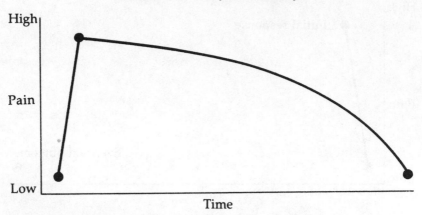

Most transitions fall somewhere in between these two extremes. Let's look at a few.

A Personal Illustration—Harry Woodward

My Golden Age was working and teaching in an academic environment. I enjoyed the image: ivy covered walls, leather patches on the jacket elbows. And even though I chose to make the change to a business environment, I felt somehow that it was not really my choice—that life, or the economy, or money was dictating it. So I started to hold the corporation for which I was working, and business in general, responsible for the fact that I had been pulled out of an environment I liked. The "ending" was handled poorly simply because I wouldn't let go of my attachment to academic life. I kept associating with university people, thinking about how I would get back there, badmouthing the business environment. Consequently, I sustained a high level of pain and discomfort. After a year, I allowed the pain to come down a little, but not all the way. I continued to engage in passive-aggressive behavior in the new environment, becoming an iconoclast, not towing the company line, and taking pride in being a maverick.

This counter-productive, hanging-on behavior came to a point where it started to interfere with my productivity on my new job. Yet I continued to sustain it, even though the company was trying to make me feel comfortable. I told them, in effect, "No, I'm just not going to let you off that easy." Then one day, I realized I wasn't hurting the company. I was only hurting myself, and it was rather silly to continue like that, not to mention the fact that I had learned a lot, acclimated to the new environment, and begun to see opportunities in it. When I realized what I was doing, the pain level dropped very quickly. But I had sustained it at such a high level for such a long time that it was a classic example of an ending handled poorly. A chart of my transition would look like that represented in Figure 5.

A Personal Illustration—Steve Buchholz

I had an opportunity to work in a different role during a dramatic corporate change. There were many pros and cons to the new job, primarily more responsibility for people who were professionals but stung by the change events. It offered new challenges, new responsibilities, and it allowed me to use certain of my abilities more, a definite plus. On the other hand, I liked certain things about the old role, including the schedule and the people I worked with. It was a difficult decision.

I decided to make the move. At that point I made a list of specific things I'd have to stop doing and specific things I'd have to start doing. And the things that I would have to stop doing required endings that were painful, severing certain relationships with people and abandoning certain activities that

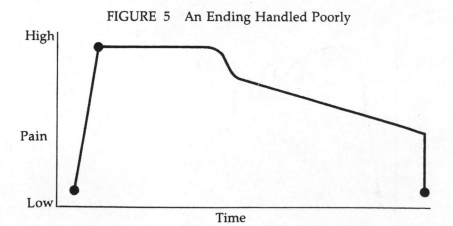

FIGURE 5   An Ending Handled Poorly

I was comfortable with and certain talents I was rewarded for.
I decided to give myself permission to mourn the loss of those
things, but promised myself that the challenge was the future
and required all my energy.

The way I did that was to remember what was ending fondly
and also to see the connections between what was ending and
what was beginning. I chose to view some of the new, totally
different job duties as opportunities rather than threats.

I allowed myself a transition period to (1) mourn and (2)
become acclimated to the new job. Although it wasn't quite
as easy as I had planned, and there was some pain and some
sorrow in that whole process, it took only a few weeks for me
to return to a position of stability and focus. And it was
primarily because of an attitude of saying, "Yes, those were
nice things and I'll mourn them, but I won't overdo it. Yes,
there are new things that are potentially threatening, but
there are also opportunities, even if I don't seen them as
fully right now as I will in the future. I'm dedicated to their
fulfillment." This mental decision provided the motivation
to move that department to new goals. At the end of the
year, we were presented the President's Award for Best
Department.

The chart for this transition would look like that in Figure
6. Superimposing the two experiences, you can see a great
difference (Figure 7). The shaded area represents how much
more difficult Harry's transition was than Steve's. (It should

FIGURE 6   An Ending Handled Well

FIGURE 7   Differences in Handling Endings

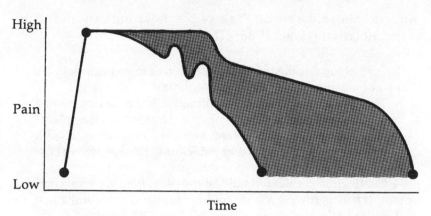

be noted that Harry *has* had some good transitions in his life and Steve some bad ones.)

The difference between these two transitions helps shed light on potential difficulties and opportunities in a changing environment. In any organization, the transition profiles for individuals and for departments will vary widely, just as in these two illustrations.

What this means is that some employees will still be fighting the change long after others have decided to move with it. In the Averco example, it looks as though Warren, left to his own devices, will stretch his line out much longer than Judy or Peggy. And Paul? Who knows what his will look like. The longer the lines, the less quickly the department as a whole will return to a high level of productivity and morale.

What does it take to shorten the line? What can you do for the people who work for you and with you to lessen the difficulty of the ending? The best way to answer is to recall the exercise you just participated in and ask: When you were in the midst of your ending—at the point of highest pain, anger, or discomfort—what would you have liked most? What would have helped?

The answers to these questions form the basis for the strategies this book advocates. To frame these strategies, move now to the *Change Model*, the stages of which have already been informally introduced: *Endings, Transitions,* and *Beginnings.*

INTRODUCTION TO THE CHANGE MODEL

An article headline reads: "Tale of plant-closing may end with different twist" (Hage, 1986). The article:*

> Today's column is the workplace version of man-bites-dog. It's a plant-closing story with a happy ending.
>
> The tale begins in Mankato, Minnesota, at a factory owned by Continental Can Co. It has all the elements of other plant-closing tragedies: an aging plant, low-cost competitors, a work force mostly older than 50 and a declining market among customers who sell canned peas and meats.
>
> Continental considered pulling the plug, then took a second look. It had a growing market for beer cans and soft-drink cans. It wanted a factory in the Upper Midwest. The plant's 99 machinists in Mankato were loyal and hard-working. "It wasn't anything the plant was doing wrong that caused the problem," said plant manager Michael Owen. "We hated to lose this work force simply because we're in a highly competitive line of cans."
>
> Continental decided to gut the plant, completely refit it and reopen it to make pop-top lids for beverage cans. First it asked for the cooperation of Lodge 924 of the International Association of Machinists, whose members would have to learn new skills and work schedules. Then Continental approached the state of Minnesota and won a $30,000 training grant from the Minnesota Job Skills Partnership. Then the company began pouring millions of dollars into new technology and $58,000 of its own into retraining the workers.
>
> The old can line ground to a halt October 20. It will resume operation early next spring, with computers and 99 machinists who will have spent the interim at a Mankato vocational-technical school learning new skills.
>
> "It's exactly what we're trying to accomplish, getting to current workers before a company pulls out, then giving them the opportunity to get the training they need," said Monica Manning, executive director of the Job Skills Partnership, which distributes state funds for training programs that match workers' skills with employers' needs.
>
> Still, the decision wasn't automatic for Lodge 924, whose members were asked to give up their five-day, 40-hour week.

*Printed with the permission of the *Minneapolis Star and Tribune,* November 25, 1986, p. 7B.

Because Continental wants the new machinery to run continuously, the machinists will work 12-hour shifts, four days on
and four days off.

Many workers also were anxious about returning to
school and facing a lot of new math and technical training,
said Richard Keltgen, president of Lodge 924. But the south-
ern Minnesota economy didn't seem to offer many jobs that
would match the $24,000 to $40,000 that machinists earned
at Continental.

"Looking around, facing cold hard reality, the food business just looked awful shaky to us," Keltgen said. "I'm sure
we'll come out on top in the end."

Maybe it is not a happy ending. Maybe it is a happy beginning.

In addition to being a classic example of Late Phase II, early
Phase III issues, the experience of the workers at Continental
Can is an example of a modern-day fairy tale—one in which
instead of everybody living happily ever after, they are able to
move successfully from what seems like a disaster to what
promises to be a future. The workers in this case experience
an *ending*—the closing of their plant. And then they move
through an uncertain *transition* which demands creativity and
the bending of a few rules to a new *beginning*. In this regard,
the Continental Can story is a clear illustration of the Change
Model.

The company was able to end their attachment to an entrenched way of life, tolerate and endure the period of ambiguity, and thereby make a successful transition to working out
the details of their vision of the new beginning.

THE BASIS OF THE CHANGE MODEL

In his book, *Transitions: Making Sense of Life's Changes,* William
Bridges proposes a three-phase process of individual change:
first comes an ending, followed by movement through a neutral zone, and then new beginnings. At each stage, Bridges
identifies a set of psychological tasks individuals need to
successfully complete in order to accept change and move
forward.

In the *ending phase,* Bridges explains, individuals first need
to *disengage.* This process may involve an actual physical move

such as changing from one job to another. Next the individual needs to *disidentify* or become *disenchanted* with the former way of doing things.

Expanding this idea, Tichy and Ulrich (1984) suggest that Chrysler, GM, AT&T, and U.S. Steel employees who cling to the "good old days" must become disenchanted with those feelings; their managers must help them "replace past glories with future opportunities. . . . Holding on to past accomplishments and memories without coming to grips with failure and the need to change may be why companies such as W.T. Grant, International Harvester, and Braniff were unsuccessful at revitalization. There is a sense of dying in all endings, and it does not help to treat transitions as if the past can be buried without effort."

Bridges' *neutral zone,* or what this book terms *transitions,* may appear to be an unproductive "time out," but according to Tichy and Ulrich it is really, "A time of reorientation where individuals complete endings and begin new patterns of behavior." But these transitions are far from easy. As Tichy and Ulrich go on to explain:

> Major transitions unleash powerful conflicting forces in people. The change invokes simultaneous positive and negative personal feelings of fear and hope, anxiety and relief, pressure and stimulation, leaving the old and accepting a new direction, loss of meaning and new meaning, threat to self-esteem and new sense of value.

Because of this difficulty, Western culture typically tries to avoid this experience and "treats the neutral zone like a busy street, to be crossed as fast as possible and certainly not a place to contemplate and experience. However, running across the neutral zone too hurriedly does not allow the ending to occur nor the new beginning to properly start." They cite as an example, Archie McGill who "was known to rant and rave about the stodgy, old fashioned, and noninnovative 'bell-shaped men' at AT&T." Although he was trying to help the company become more innovative and market oriented, Tichy and Ulrich suspect "he may not have allowed them to accept the endings inherent in the transition. Although his enthusiasm may have been well placed, he may have lacked the sensitivity to individual endings and neutral phases of transitions."

Tichy and Ulrich summarize *new beginnings* like this:

> After individuals accept endings by working through neutral zones, they are able to work with new enthusiasm and commitment. New beginnings are characterized by employees learning from the past rather than reveling in it, looking for new scripts rather than acting out old ones, and being positive and excited about current and future work opportunities rather than dwelling on past successes or failures.

The Change Model describes the reaction to change in three terms: endings, transitions, and beginnings.

BASIC PREMISES OF THE CHANGE MODEL

When change occurs, some things *end*. They cease to be. These endings are often painful or confusing, and before people can move on they must come to terms with the changes and resolve them. If they do not, they will be unable to let go of the past and will carry excess emotional baggage with them into the new venture.

Transitions are a time of weaning people from the old to the new. These transitions require that you become conscious of what is ending and what is beginning. Transitions are also the times when you will probably need more support from your friends and colleagues and when, in turn, you will need to provide more support for the members of your work unit.

Once you have phased into the new, you are faced with the challenge of *beginnings*. At this point, you must align yourself on a common purpose and vision.

The Change Model—An Aerial View

One way to understand the Change Model and the integral interrelationship of its three parts is to compare it with a trapeze artist. Picture a "flyer" swinging back and forth on a circus trapeze. When he comes to the height of his arc, he lets go, turns around in mid air, and—what does he want to have there? Another trapeze or a strong pair of hands. When trapeze artists perform, they are so confident of each other's abilities that the "flyer" can let go and turn around with complete faith that a trapeze or a "catcher" is going to be there. But let's say you are put in the place of the "flyer"; you have never "flown" before, and you are not sure if anything's going to be there when you let go. To make the situation even more difficult, there is no net below you. How likely are you to let go of that trapeze? Not very. Even if your own trapeze rope is fraying, you will probably hang on to that trapeze, because if you go down, at least you will be holding on to something.

It is hard to let go and turn around in mid air with faith that something will be there. What you have to do if you are not sure, is to look over your shoulder or to let go with one hand and grab for the catcher with the other. In any case, most people see change as endings and beginnings—flying from one trapeze to another. Something ends and then you have to suddenly go on and begin something new which requires letting go in mid air and jumping for what you hope is going to be there. That is the function of the transition part of the process. It helps you turn your head or reach out your arm, or do whatever it takes to make that transition to the new thing. Hanging on, refusing to let go of the trapeze is the consummate example of a "bad ending"—you are unwilling to part with that thing that you've been attached to.

One central issue of change is that when you move into Phase III, the future—the beginning—is not predictable. As a result, people are asked to let go and hang in mid air a while with the promise that something positive will appear.

ENDINGS

During the change process, you are in the position, either voluntarily or involuntarily, of having to end an attachment to an old way of doing things. You actually have to stop doing things one way and begin doing them another.

Endings are typically viewed in terms of losses. One kind of perceived loss is job loss: "I used to have this particular job, but now I don't." If a company changes to a market-driven approach, for example, employees who had recordkeeping or procedural jobs may suddenly have jobs that require them to communicate with customers. These employees often perceive that their old jobs have been done away with—their technical skills have been sidetracked—and that they are now being forced to do something for which they are unprepared. That is not really true; their jobs have just been expanded. But whenever you change someone's job description, the employee may experience it initially as loss.

A second perceived loss has to do with people: "I used to work with these people, and now I'm cut off," or, "I used to work on this team, and now I'm no longer a member of the team." Eventually these people will probably form new friendships and new teams, but the sense of loss is great at the point of change; they identified with people, a group of fellow workers, or a department that has been taken away.

A third perceived loss associated with endings is the loss of familiar methods and procedures. This loss is closely related to the job loss, but it has to do with what people *do* as opposed to their titles. They feel competent in doing certain things; suddenly their jobs are changed or expanded and they feel less competent. Although not everything has changed, and they will learn the new methods and procedures, they feel like novices. This leads them to believe in a somewhat exaggerated way that they are no longer effective or secure.

Too often people have the idea that in a change situation something old or comfortable totally ends and another totally new thing begins. Most often, however, only a small portion of the job actually changes, but the perception is that "my whole" job has changed. In fact, a study asked how much of somebody's job you had to change before that person perceived that the entire job had been changed. The result: You change 15 to 20 percent of somebody's job, and they perceive that the "whole" job has changed.

In the Averco example in the last chapter, Rick's announcement to his people gives a glimpse of what might be termed the beginning of the ending. Except for Peggy and possibly Dennis, all the others are reacting to a felt loss. You do not know specifically what these perceived losses are yet. That information surfaces in later chapters. Now you see only the symptoms: Anger, confusion, worry, and withdrawal. It doesn't take much deduction to conclude, however, that if these emotions are not dealt with, either by the people experiencing them or by someone else, they will be carried over as excess emotional baggage and interfere with the transitions and beginnings process.

Excess Baggage

How do people carry excess baggage into the new venture? What does that look like when they get into the new situation? The most overt emotional carryovers are lingering anger, resentment, worry, confusion, or withdrawal. In these instances, the initial response is maintained at near full strength. It dominates the person's activity and reduces his or her effectiveness. People in effect vow, "I won't let them forget," or "I'll show them it won't work," or "This is never going to be clear."

If the initial reaction fades, however, the excess baggage can express itself in more subtle ways such as noncompliance or passive-aggressive and antisocial behavior.

If people perceive loss of a job, as in the example of employees familiar with clerical tasks who suddenly had to communicate with the public, they will tend to stress the clerical part of their new job and not be enthusiastic, or in fact may not even perform the part of their new jobs that deals with the public. They will have quit and stayed, putting in time but not giving their full energy to the organization.

If people perceive that they have lost a team or a group in the change, they may be reluctant to make new friends or establish new relationships with new groups or teams. Rather, they will tend to associate with their old friends, sit with them at lunch, continuously return to the friend or team and reminisce. In other words, they keep their emotional friendship ties to the people they have left and do not develop them in the new area. They become the marginal or "odd" persons in the new group.

If the perceived loss is in terms of methods and procedures, the reaction may be similar to that of perceived job loss. Sometimes, when people's job methodologies change, they simply do not use the new methods. They continue to use the old ones, even after they are told over and over again to change.

In other words, the excess baggage is typically not stopping—not ending that familiar job, personal relationship, method, or procedure, but continuing to do it or keep it in the new situation.

INTELLECTUAL VERSUS EMOTIONAL ENDINGS

Endings are often painful and disorienting. Even though you may fully realize, intellectually, that the ending is necessary or inevitable, it still hurts to let go. In short, during endings:

- The "known" ceases.
- It happens quickly or slowly.
- You choose it or it is forced on you.
- You give your intellectual consent.
- You have emotional reactions, frequently negative.

This final point is one of the most important. Just because you can understand something doesn't mean you accept it. But people try to convince themselves that intellectual understanding equals emotional acceptance, and then they can't understand why they are still feeling upset. Think of the analogy of the organ transplant mentioned earlier. A patient can fully understand in his mind that the new kidney is needed, but his immune system fights it nevertheless.

Similarly, our emotions often operate independently of our thought processes. The result? Emotional reservations tend to draw energy. If you have electricity flowing into a house, but it is being drawn off by something else, that diminishes the amount of electricity reaching the outlets. Likewise, emotional reservations drain off energy that could otherwise be used productively.

**Emotional reservations result in a
constant energy drain.**

Consequently, people in change often have a sense of fatigue that seems out of proportion to the amount of external effort they are putting out.

It is critical in the whole change process to understand the difference between intellectual acceptance and emotional reservations. Our culture teaches us to intellectualize, to think and logic and reason. "If you can understand it, then you can deal with it." In contrast, you are not given a lot of skills to help you deal with emotional reservations. Yet they are the ones that can cause the most trouble in the change process.

When talking with people who work for you or with you, you will probably have people tell you, "No problem." But you can see that there *is* a problem. Or maybe you cannot. One of the worst aspects of change is that people take their emotions underground, either because they want to hide their displeasure, are afraid of the consequences of expressing it, or have not fully faced up to their true feelings. They can become caught up in rumor, innuendo, malicious compliance, or even sabotage—all the while maintaining a positive face to management and fellow employees.

Another aspect of this dichotomy is that people will express emotional concerns in intellectual or technical jargon. They might say, for example, that the change is a bad idea when they are really feeling a sense of loss because their team has been taken away. But their statement, "This is a bad idea," or "This isn't efficient," is more socially acceptable than saying, "I miss that old gang of mine," or "I'm scared." In other words, people tend to translate their raw, emotional concerns into more socially acceptable, intellectual, or technical statements. Thus when dealing with people in a changing environment, it is often necessary to translate the stated "technical" objection back into the emotional content which is at its core. If you do not, if you simply address the technical issue, you may think you have resolved it only to have it flare up again as yet another "technical" objection somewhere else. Treating symptoms does not work.

Think back to the "Never End/Golden Age" exercise at the beginning of this chapter. Recall your emotions when something you did not want to end *did* end. If it was a painful experience, why? What was your sense of loss? What were you hanging on to?

It often takes some mental gear shifting to answer these questions. People often *experience* deep emotions but do *not* understand them. True, they have the ability, as mentioned earlier, to disguise their emotional reservations as technical objections, but these objections are merely rationalizations. For this reason, pushing yourself and others to identify, specifically, the losses and the respective "trapezes"—those things people refuse to let go of—is the key to the ending process. Only then can you identify exactly what you are hanging on to and then begin the process of letting go and moving on.

TRANSITIONS

The process of letting go and moving on is called transition. The logical question is, transition to what? It is difficult enough to let go, but it is doubly difficult if there is not something there to hang on to or at least reach for. Recall the trapeze.

The transition is not so much seeing the future as good, but taking what is good from the past into that future. Granted, you cannot repeat the past, but that does not mean you cannot make certain applications or connections. The ending is not so much in the tasks or the experiences as it is in the emotions, the attachments. The actual skills, the ones you are leaving behind or expanding, may have a bridging quality. Very often, you can find your new identity and make it stronger in a new situation by seeing the connection between your strengths in the old situation. It is not as if 100 percent of your job or life ends and then 100 percent of your new job or life starts. It is more like 15 to 25 percent ends, and with the remaining 85 to 75 percent you have to make the connections to the new.

In organizations, this period of making connections can be very trying. It may involve extensive retraining, many false starts and reorganizations, and a lot of ambiguity. It may take years before the beginning feels comfortable. As a result, organizations in change do not have maps, only compasses. No one knows exactly where the road will lead or whether it is the right road. They can only point the direction, move, and make midcourse corrections as needed.

The key to transitions is to make the link between the old and the new and to clarify a direction and a goal. Even if these objectives are only sketchy at first, they still represent something to head for. Letting go is easier when you know there is something else there to reach for.

Think again of the Averco work unit. Making links and clarifying a direction is precisely what Rick did *not* do. His meeting was more a wake than a wedding. Following his lead, the unit members concentrated more on their emotions than on clarifying losses or looking for connections.

This pronouncement is not meant as much as a criticism of Rick and his work unit as it is a depiction of an event that commonly occurs when organizations undergo change. But it does raise the question, "What should they have done? What would have worked?"

Never End Revisited

You may recall that at the end of the Never End exercise, you were asked to consider the question, "When you were in the midst of your initial reaction, at the point of highest discomfort in your change, what would have helped?" (Or, indeed, what *did* help?) Many people have responded to that question. The most common responses are:

- To receive understanding and empathy.
- To clarify *why* I am stuck.
- To let go and get unstuck.
- To begin to connect the old with the new.
- To focus on new beginnings.

Reducing these needs further, three basic things appear to help people through change.

- **Empathy**   Someone to listen and allow you, without judgment, to express your feelings and thoughts.
- **Information**   An intellectual understanding of what happened. What am I hanging on to? What is my sense of loss?
- **Ideas**   Suggestions for action, options, plans.
  Interestingly, some people want empathy first and informa-

tion second. Others want information first and *then* someone to listen. Whichever seems best, the point is clear. People want to meet emotional and intellectual needs *before* considering ideas and suggestions. People seem to prefer a chance to work through their feelings and thoughts *before* they take action. Unfortunately, in changing environments, people are too often pushed prematurely into taking action. Organizations, managers, and employees in change tend, as mentioned, to jump to beginnings. As a result, what people in change want is not what they usually get. More specifically, what they actually get is:

- **Autocratic behavior**   Suggestions, tasks, orders; often well-meant and reasonable, but directive nevertheless.
- **Avoidance**   The absence of empathy and listening. Some managers and other employees actively avoid talking about feelings because they are uncomfortable with them. Others rationalize, saying, "We're here to work, not to do counseling" or "If you want to have your feelings at home, fine. But when you come here, leave them at the door. This is a *business!*" Still others, because of the press of activities during change, simply do not have time for or do not think about others' feelings. In any case, the result is the same; the person feels that nobody is listening or identifying with his or her concerns.
- **Rah rah**   Classic jumping-to-beginnings, "Let's get the troops fired up" behavior. Ignore the problems, full-steam ahead. Although some form of this activity is appropriate in the beginnings phase, it is highly resented as a means of transition.

IN SUMMARY

What people in change want:	What people in change usually get:
Empathy	Autocratic behavior
Information	Avoidance
Ideas	Rah rah

The path to successful organizational transitions is to reverse this situation, to help people get what they need and
avoid what they do not need. But organizations in change,
by their nature, tend to gravitate to those things on the right.
Thus, it becomes a job for individuals to buck the tide of an
organization's habitual way of dealing with change and intervene in ways which are more productive and beneficial. The
key is balance, knowing what to do and when.

True transitions are difficult to chart. They begin in endings
and end in beginnings. But they play a vital role in making the
change process work and moving on to the new beginnings.

BEGINNINGS

Organizations think beginnings long before people do. The result is a conflict between organizational impetus and the critical mass to make it happen. The result, as you have seen, is an
employee sense of being pushed or cajoled into the new system.
Or shamed. Unable to appreciate the need for endings and transitions, the organization may label these activities as inappropriate and the people as unmotivated or trouble makers.

To truly have a beginning, there must be a certain level of
general ownership of the change. This ownership comes only
after people are well along the way through their transition.
But not everybody is at the same place. And in most changing
environments, there is not one change, but a series of changes.
As a result, people are not only at different places, but are
continually changing places—moving ahead to a beginning
only to be thrown back to endings by yet another reorganization or new policy.

For these reasons, beginnings cannot afford to rely on what
many insiders consider to be the building blocks of beginnings,
namely goals, plans, and motivation. Those are managerial
"pushing" activities. Rather beginnings, especially in their
early stages, must rely on vision, commitment, and alignment
on purpose—those elements that are leadership, "drawing"
activities.

Vision, commitment, alignment on purpose—these are
grand ideals. But are they practical? Are they "do-able"? The
answer is "Yes." However lofty they may sound, there are,

nevertheless, practical ways to accomplish them. In later chapters you will learn strategies to remove these activities from their pedestals and practical ways to implement them.

Before beginnings can start, however, organizations must establish trust. If trust is not established, beginning activities will remain at the level of hype and hypocrisy. The most effective way to build this trust is to give credence to the aspects of the Change Model that precede beginnings—endings and transitions.

ORGANIZATIONS AND THE CHANGE MODEL

When asked to list the activities of change, people in organizations, not surprisingly, mention organizing, planning, holding meetings, writing memos, getting people "on board" and fired up, rebudgeting, scheduling training, and, in general, activity.

When you examine this list in light of the Change Model, it quickly becomes apparent that 70 to 80 percent of those things listed are beginning activities. Such an exercise is a good way to help people see their own and their organization's tendency to jump to beginnings. This exercise also begs the question, why? If this tendency increases rather than decreases the discomfort of change, why do people do it?

One obvious factor is time. People want to move on. Employees and managers are supposed to be proactive, moving forward, doing things, not thinkers or dawdlers. They are supposed to have themselves intellectually and emotionally together.

Unfortunately, if you try to jump to beginnings or force others to jump to beginnings, then you have neglected a very important part of the whole change process, namely transitions and endings. As mentioned, however, these endings can come back to haunt you. Therefore, the first step in the Change Model requires reflection and understanding. Managers and employees must understand their own emotional reactions to the change as well as the emotional reactions of the individuals who work with them. They need people skills to move through endings and transitions to new beginnings.

In this book, the focus is on the front of the model—more on endings and transitions than on beginnings. The rationale for this approach is quite simple. The need is for a focus on endings and transitions because those are the areas most neglected. Although you may buy into this approach intellectually, the actual practice of it will be much more difficult. By adopting this approach, you will, in many ways, be going against the grain of the culture you find yourself in. The pressures to jump to beginnings will be felt. This is not to say that you should stop work for a week and immerse yourself into deep counseling. That's not necessary. The skills and strategies you will learn are simple and immediately applicable.

A FINAL POINT

Often people ask if the Change Model is anything like the Death and Dying Model used by Elizabeth Kübler-Ross and others. At first our initial response was "No." To compare change and death seemed a little heavy. But the more we thought about it, the more we realized that the process was, indeed, very similar. In many ways it is identical to it, especially in light of the fact that the death and dying model has more recently been genericized to the "Loss Model."

The basic premise of the Loss Model is that when loss occurs, the people who remain have to go through some basic stages—denial, anger, bargaining, depression—to finally achieve acceptance. The premise of the model is that one must move *through* the stages, not skip them and try to jump to acceptance. This process helps you move through those stages as opposed to getting bogged down in the mourning, anger, or denial stages.

Likewise, a basic premise in this book is that you experience certain stages during change. To try to skip the endings and transitions stages and jump to beginnings is an error. People may intellectually be in step with you, but emotionally, they are going to be back in endings. The intent of the tactics presented in this book is to help people move through the stages more quickly than they might otherwise.

4

THE EFFECTS OF CHANGE: THE CHANGE RESPONSE SCALE

Some people learn from their experiences;
others never recover.

If you think you know how people are
feeling, you're probably wrong.
So what you have to do is ask them.
Now when you do that, you're going to
find out things you don't want to hear,
but you get some pleasant surprises
too. But whatever you get is a better
basis for working through the change
than just guessing.
Manager in a Changing Environment

To this point, you have looked at the inevitability of change; the formative, normative, and integrative phases of growth businesses go through (represented by the Growth Curve); and the Endings, Transitions, and Beginnings people go through during change (depicted by the Change Model).

You have also looked at the tendency in people and in organizations to jump to beginnings. No sooner is the reorganization or new marketing strategy announced than task forces and committees are established to implement them—to take action—regardless of how people are reacting or the endings they are experiencing. When endings and transitions are neglected, however, serious problems can result.

Each area of the Change Model poses a key question. Focus now on the first segment of the Change Model: Endings. The key question here is:

How does change affect my co-workers and me?

Notice in this statement the emphasis is not on what you should *do*. Instead, it encourages observation, asking yourself how you and the people you work with are reacting to the change. These reactions can range from anger, confusion, and frustration to passive acceptance and enthusiastic support. Asking this question is analogous to taking a temperature. The diagnosis and plan of action come later.

The scale for this temperature-taking process is a simple scale from 1 to 10; 1 is resisting change, 5 is not supporting but not resisting it, and 10 is completely supporting it.

To help in the observation process, you can also use certain pairs of words to put at either end of the scale: victim/owner, loss/gain, and rigidity/resilience.

VICTIM/OWNER

Victim may seem like a strong word, but used in a change context it denotes people who feel that the change was done *to* them. Unless people are allowed to process endings and move through transitions, they tend to see themselves as victimized by events beyond their control. The key word in the victim's thinking is "they." "Well, *they* did it to us again." Or "Why didn't *they* tell us?"

Victims perceive that they have no choice in the change and certainly no ownership of it. Rather, they feel that they have no option but to wait for the next dictate or turn of events, hope for the best, but expect the worst.

In organizations, victims are often the resisters and detractors. Or they may sink into noncompliance and inaction. Whatever their behavior, their energy is being drawn away from any kind of productive activity and channeled into negative emotions.

Individuals responding as *owners* of the change take a different position. They are active participants in the change rather than passive bystanders. They may or may not like the change or agree that it is for the best, but whatever their feelings, these people are at least willing to work toward implementing the change, saying, "I have some reservations about this, but I'll try to deal with it on its own terms." Ownership can occur on a continuum from positive to neutral to negative.

Positive ownership occurs when the person is willing not only to give the change a chance, but shows some level of commitment to making it work. If they are in favor of the change, you might hear, "I think it's a good idea and I'll work for it."

But even if they have reservations, people can still take a positive approach. In this case, you might hear, "I don't agree with this change, but I don't want to be an obstructionist. I'll work toward implementing it, but I reserve the right to gripe and to try to change other things as we go along."

However negative this last statement may appear, it is important to realize that although voicing disagreement, here is a person who is actively involved in trying to make *something* work.

Neutral ownership characterizes the person who is not committed but who will at least comply. This person might say, "Well, this is the way it is, and it's yet to be seen if it will work, but I'm willing to give it a chance." Neutral ownership is basically a wait-and-see position.

Negative ownership is basically resignation. This person says, "Well, what's done is done. The decision's been made, so we might as well get on with it." Although perilously close to a victim stance, this person is still at least willing to *work with* rather than *oppose* or sabotage the change.

These statements all reflect ownership, although the speakers vary on whether they *agree* with what is going on.

**People can own something and still
not agree with it.**

LOSS/GAIN

Some people tend to resist change because they perceive that they will lose more than they will gain. Although there are both losses and gains in most situations, these people tend to focus on the loss and lose sight of the gain. Others embrace the change because they see that the gain is greater than the potential loss. Which of these two perceptions a person adopts will depend to a great extent on how that person deals with endings and transitions.

The loss/gain perception may be the simplest, yet most useful distinction in reaction to change. People can quickly answer the question, "What do you feel you have lost or will lose in this change?" They can rattle off a whole list of perceived losses: loss of identity, loss of a promotion path, loss of a team, loss of a desirable location, loss of competence, and the like. Often many of these losses may never actually occur.

This fear is sometimes called the Boogey Man syndrome. In changing environments, rumors build upon themselves, becoming larger and more catastrophic, "I hear they're going to cut another 10 percent," or "The management committee's meeting again today, and you remember what happened the last time they met." These rumors spread quickly and also become more credible, so that in a short time people actually believe that the Boogey Man's coming and he is going to get them. As one worker put it, "It ain't the things you don't know what gets you into trouble. It's the things you know for sure what ain't so."

On the other hand, ask these same people what they feel they will gain from the change and three basic responses are likely. The first is, "Nothing." Often people are hit so hard by change, they can't see any gains at all. A second response is, "Well, let's see—I guess I could . . ." This response requires people to mentally shift gears, but once they do, they are able to see the change in terms of options and possible opportunities. A final response is, "Gains? Certainly. There are a lot of things to gain." How similar a person's response is to the first, second, or third example gives you some idea where he or she may be on an overall 1–10 Change Scale.

Identifying both gains *and* losses is a very valuable exercise in a changing environment. The gains, obviously, will help people move on. But identifying losses can also serve as the initial step in a bridge-building process. Focusing on losses may seem at first to be negative, and to be sure, *dwelling* on losses will probably not be very productive. But identifying specific losses can be valuable for two reasons. One, it may clarify a feeling or belief that on closer examination can be shown to be false. Two, it may identify something very important to that person—a skill, a promotion path, affiliation—which, although it will cease to exist in the present organization, may be able to be re-established in another form in the new organization.

One person, for example, was the head of a department that was phased out. From a position of importance, he was now feeling a loss of position, job function, and prestige. He felt betrayed and assumed that if he even *had* a job in the new organization, he would have to "start over." Others in the organization saw him, however, not in terms of his job and position as much as in terms of his organizational and leadership abilities. Thus they saw possibilities where he did not. Only when the employee was able to see that with some retraining in a new system he could again be a department head, did he begin to focus on gains and move through the change. In other words, only when he focused on his losses—his generic skills as a manager and leader, skills he thought he was losing—was he able to see connections between what he was doing and what he *could* be doing.

RIGIDITY (FORM)/RESILIENCE (PURPOSE)

The third set of scale determinants is rigidity/resilience. Rigidity is basically an attachment to form such as a procedure, guideline, system, or way of doing things. On the other hand, resilience signifies focus on purpose, on the end result.

In change situations, people may respond from a position of rigidity because they are attached to the form or the original structure, rather than to the overall purpose the form is designed to serve. Those people who respond from a position of resilience are focused on the purpose of the change.

Consider what might happen if a plant became automated. Rigid employees would want to go back to the old system because it provided satisfaction, self-worth, comfort, security, and stability. They would resist the automation and remain attached to the *form* of the old system because of the fear that the new form would not provide the same satisfaction.

Resilient employees, in contrast, would focus on the *purpose* of the change, not on the form. The purpose of the automation is to increase efficiency, make the company more competitive, insure its survival, and in the long run, increase profits that will be beneficial to all employees. The form or structure is of less significance—the purpose is what counts.

Enright (1984) suggests that individuals functioning from a position of rigidity, or what he terms "solidity," focus on resistance to change: "We've always done it this way." "This product has been a winner; let's not change it." "Joe's good at that task." Boundaries and turf become important, as does getting better and better at more specialized tasks. He contrasts this with the "resilient" or "versatile" mode where change is accepted as a challenge. Major differences between these two modes are summarized in Figure 1 on page 73.

Tichy (1983) has compiled a list of technical, political, and cultural system resistances that are conducive to rigidity. Among the technical system resistances are habit and inertia, fear of the unknown or loss of organizational predictability,

FIGURE 1   The Cultures of Solidity and Resilience

There are clusters of attitudes and values that are more supportive of resilience/versatility and others more supportive of the tendency to look for security in outside, solid forms.

	Culture of Solidity	Culture of Resilience
Some Primary Virtues and Values:	Polished, finished Predictable Specialized skills Values clarity Elaborate planning	Room for more development Versatile General abilities Values scope Skill at improvising
In education:	Values degrees, certificates, licenses	Values substance of education and training
Prefers:	Formal arrangements (contracts, tenure) Familiar environments	Informal arrangements (independent consultant) New environments
Emphasis:	Means and procedures Process (means) Letter of the law Power through hierarchy Control reality People should fit jobs Turf and jurisdiction	Values and mission Results (ends) Spirit of the law Influence through networks Accept reality Jobs should fit people Relevance and convenience
Slogans:	"Polish and perfect it." "Let's do it right!"	"Master it and move on." "Let's get it to work!"
Lives in:	Tradition and past	Present
View of Mistake:	It's bad; things must be going wrong. It means failure.	Necessary sign that chances are being taken. "Failure is incomplete learning."
View of Success:	Good sign that things are going well. Desired state.	Mixed blessing. Not enough chances being taken. "Success is a missed opportunity to learn something new."

and sunk costs. Political system resistances include powerful coalitions, resource limitations, and leaders having to indict their own past decisions and behaviors. Cultural system resistances include selective perception (cultural filters), security based on the past, and a lack of climate for change. Appendix A contains an elaboration of these resistances.

IN SUMMARY

When change occurs, people and procedures are "tossed in the air," and they all land somewhere on a continuum between each of the three paired reactions just described (Figure 2). They feel like either victims or owners, losers or winners. They adopt an attitude either of rigidity or resilience.

Use of the Scale

More than just an intellectual construct, the scale can be a very useful tool in the early stages of a change. Consider the people in Rick's department at Averco Corporation. The initial meeting between Rick and his people was the event that threw the department up in the air. The reactions ranged all the way from Peggy's, "That's great!" to Warren's walking out; from Judy's, "I've got some questions," to Paul's clamming up and saying, "Fine"; from Dennis's worry to Rick's frustration. So where is the department? How are people reacting?

The first impression, in spite of some positive comments, is that the situation is negative. Left at this general conclusion— negative—the environment would be ripe for rumor, self-fulfilling prophecies, and Boogey-Man invention. But what are the people in that department *really* feeling—as individuals?

Answering this question is critical. Determining "How does change affect my co-workers and me?" or better, "How *is* it affecting us?" is a question that has to be answered both specifically and quickly. You want to answer it specifically because when people are forced to face up to their losses and gains, they often find that there are fewer losses than they thought and more gains than they originally saw. You want to answer it quickly to break the back of the rumor mill before it starts to build up momentum.

Using the Change Response Scale is the first step in this process. It can be used by individuals and departments to get a reading on where people have "come down" regarding the change; it can be used by managers to develop a strategy for dealing with people in their departments. The more people in a department or on a team, the more useful the scale.

On the following pages, you will have the opportunity to use this scale to make determinations about Rick and the

FIGURE 2

The Change Response Scale

Moving Away From Change	0	2	4	6	8	10	Moving Toward Change

	0	2	4	6	8	10	
Victim	0	2	4	6	8	10	Owner
Loss	0	2	4	6	8	10	Gain
Rigidity (Form)	0	2	4	6	8	10	Resilience (Purpose)

people in his department. Before beginning that process, however, you need to revisit an issue touched on earlier: technical versus emotional concerns.

TECHNICAL VERSUS EMOTIONAL CONCERNS REVISITED

When the change is announced, Rick is confused about what to do and angry that he was not more involved. He has technical concerns about the actual mechanics of the change process, and he also has emotional concerns about how it was done and how he will tell his people.

And what about his people? Judy appears to have mainly technical concerns because she said she had a lot of questions. Peggy seems to be okay technically and emotionally. Paul does not say anything, but he is obviously quite worried about the change; you do not know anything about his technical concerns, but you do know something is bothering him. Dennis wants to be positive, but is basically guarded. Warren is mad. In fact, his anger dominates his response so completely that you do not find out much about his technical concerns.

At the beginning of a change process, the emotional concerns are much more energized than the technical ones. And even when people voice strong opinions or complaints about technical matters, the power behind them is usually emotional. Indeed, if technical issues were the only issues of change, the process would be relatively easy.

It is easier to deal with technical concerns than with emotional concerns.

Why? Technical concerns can be addressed through planning, training, objective setting, and the like. Technical concerns are more finite and predictable. Emotional concerns, on the other hand, are unpredictable, volatile, and hidden—and often go off unexpectedly like time bombs. Dealing with them involves time, listening, and counseling—the very things people perceive they do *not* have in a change situation. So they avoid or ignore these issues. Also, as noted earlier, most people in organizations get promoted because of their technical/ task-related abilities rather than their people-related skills. This does not mean that the people concerns are not important to an organization. They are. But they just seem soft when compared to the quantifiable and demonstrable technical skills, especially in a stable environment. As a result, when change hits and the importance of the technical-emotional skill balance is flipflopped, many people find themselves faced with needs they have little practice in or experience dealing with. The result of this shift, for them personally, is a sudden energy drain.

To illustrate, picture this. You get up in the morning and you begin to expend energy. You expend 1 energy unit brushing your teeth and 3 eating breakfast. You then go to work and spend an hour dealing with technical concerns and another hour dealing with emotional concerns. What do you imagine the ratio of units burned up in each of these situations would be? According to an informal poll, most people indicate 10 units for an hour's worth of technical as opposed to 40+ units for an hour's worth of emotional. The more emotional concerns there are to deal with, the more energy will be drained off.

At a strategic level, upper management can plan for the technical problems of change. But at a tactical level, first-line and middle management deal with technical *and* people problems. Often the people/management skills most in demand are those with which managers have the least experience. They need tools to deal with people in a changing environment.

One aim of the tools presented in this book is energy management. The tools are designed to enable you to use fewer units of energy in your dealings with other people. The first tool is the Change Response Scale—a tool of recognition.

The first tool or skill is that of recognition.

RECOGNIZING HOW CHANGE IS AFFECTING PEOPLE

How are people reacting? This statement is equally as important for what it *does not* say as it is for what it *does* say. It *does not* ask, "What should I do?" Rather it asks you to observe and then ask, "How am I reacting? How are other people reacting?"

Organizations tend to put a premium on *action*. This tendency contradicts what the Change Model suggests; that is, the first step should be to take a step back and look around. The business culture, however, does not lend itself to or reinforce stepping back and looking around. It reinforces action, even blind action, which in turn leads toward the syndrome of "jumping to beginnings." You will need to act, of course, but before doing so, *observe*. In short—

Focus on the reaction, not the solution.

By focusing on the reaction, you will go a long way toward insuring that the action you ultimately take will be the best action.

As people working to implement change, your role is like that of a doctor. Observe, diagnose, prescribe, and encourage practice for future prevention of problems. Start by returning to the Averco Corporation and looking at how change is affecting Rick and the members of his team.

Averco Corporation

Listen in on Rick, talking on the phone with another manager, one of his peers:

> "How'm I doing? Don't ask. How're you doing? . . . Yeah, I know. . . . Exactly, and you know what really gets me? It's like we've got to get this thing done by, like tomorrow. . . . Yeah, maybe you're right. Maybe they *will* give us 'til Friday. . . . Hey, that's the new style. Management by grenade. . . . Combining One and Four—we all knew it was going to happen. We all wanted it. But, it's just the complexity. And the quickness. . . . Hey, I'm going through the same thing. My people are coming to me and asking me questions, and I'm going blah-blah-blah-this and blah-blah-blah-that. I don't even know what I'm talking about really. And they've got a *right* to want to know. All I can say to them is, well, keep your head up and your chin down. We're counting on you. . . . We having fun yet?"

In his conversation, Rick reacts alternately to technical and emotional matters. He seems to agree with the mechanics of the change, but does not like the suddenness of its announcement and the time frame. His emotions run the gamut.

- Not feeling well—"How am I doing? Don't ask."
- Supportive—"We all wanted it."
- Stressed—"Too complex; too quick."
- Mad at management—"Management by grenade."
- Helpless—"Can't answer my people's questions."
- Ironic humor—"We having fun yet?"

Also, this conversation tells you about the "true" Rick. With his employees, Rick had to put on a front to a certain extent. But he can be open and honest with his peer. People in organizations often find themselves in a double bind. They have to deal with the problems of the change and at the same time be advocates for something to which they may not be fully committed.

If you were to rate Rick's response on a scale of 1 to 10—1 being "moving away from" or resisting change and 10 being "moving toward" or accepting change, where would you put him?

If giving Rick a "score" seems a little arbitrary or judgmental, remember, the Change Response Scale is only a first-cut observation—a tool to get a general sense of where people are. As mentioned, the scale is like taking a person's temperature or white count. It does not diagnose the illness but provides an indicator of the person's general condition. Later, you will learn in more detail about the actual uses of this scale. But for now, ask yourself the following questions, "Is Rick experiencing more gain or more loss? Is he a victim or an owner of the change? Is he coming from rigidity or resilience?" (Figure 3).

FIGURE 3   How Rick Is Affected by Change

Rick:

| Moving Away From Change | 0   2   4   6   8   10 | Moving Toward Change |

Look now at each of the other people. How are they feeling? What are their main concerns? Picture first the following scenario. Warren stalks into Rick's office.

RICK: Warren, come on in.

WARREN: Got your note.

RICK: Good. Well, what do you think?

WARREN: What do I think? You *know* what I think. It's not gonna work. *That's* what I think. (Bitterly) Does anybody have any real idea what's going on here? It's not just a matter of numbers you know. Lose One, make Four Three, and

Three's going to be Two. Come on. It's a lot more complicated than that. Doesn't anyone realize that? No one talked to me. Rick, you didn't talk to me. It's not going to work. It's inefficient. The old system works much better. Not to mention, people are not going to accept the change.

RICK: Warren, I know you're upset. But we need your creativity and your input *now*, when it counts.

WARREN: Creativity?! It doesn't count now. It counted *before*. Did anyone value my creativity or input before? Oh, no. No. Hey, Warren, here it is—fait accompli. We'll just move Three; no, maybe we'll move Two; no, we'll move One. Come on, Rick. People respect me. I know how things work, and I could have told you; you can't ramrod change like this. It's not thought out, and people will *not* accept it. They're coming to me, and I don't know *what* to tell them. They need to be able to count on me, but now—forget it.

Although Warren refers to some technical issues, declaring that the change is "inefficient" and not "thought out," the bulk of his objection seems to be around deeper personal reactions.

- Angry, hurt—"Didn't talk to me."
- Less in charge—"They used to be able to count on me."

In general, Warren's asserting, "It won't work," tells you more about Warren than the change. In reality, Warren is saying one thing and meaning something else, expressing emotional concerns in technical terminology.

Take another example. You are a manager. An employee comes to you and begins discussing what is essentially an emotional concern, but in technical language. You hear the technical language but don't read beneath; you take it at face value and deal with the person at the technical level. You think, "That's easy; we've solved that problem," only to find the person coming back with the same problem. Your response might be, "Wait a minute. I thought we already solved that." If it were just a technical matter, you would have already solved it. But since it was something deeper, you did not. So the person comes back giving the same or different technical expression for the same underlying emotional problem. If this happens, you need to stop and ask, "What is really going on here? What is the emotional content underlying the technical statement? What is the loss?" Place Warren on the Change Response Scale (Figure 4).

FIGURE 4   How Warren Is Affected by Change

Warren:

| Moving Away From Change | 0 2 4 6 8 10 | Moving Toward Change |

Next eavesdrop on a conversation over coffee among Judy, Peggy, and Paul. Judy and Peggy are involved in a discussion when Paul happens into the scene.

PEGGY: Well, I think it's great. These changes are long overdue, and it isn't like we didn't know it was coming.

JUDY: Well, maybe. But I don't know. I'm not sure how I feel. I guess I just need more information. Like, for example, are we going to have the same number of people? Have you heard?

PEGGY: I don't know, Judy. I would guess for the time being, yes.

JUDY: But later?

PEGGY: I don't know. But I think that's what *we've* got to help decide.

JUDY: Uh huh. But what about output? Are we going to have to maintain the same level of output during the changeover?

PEGGY: I think so. I mean, it'll be tough, but I think we can—

JUDY: And how about budget? Is there going to be a new budget during switchover?

PEGGY: I think there'd *have* to be. In fact, that's what I've been working on this morning, fooling around with some ideas to make this thing move more smoothly.

JUDY: Um hum.

Paul enters.

PAUL: Hi, Peggy, Judy.

PEGGY: We haven't seen you around much the last few days. That's not like you.

PAUL: Yeah, well, I've been busy.

PEGGY: Paul, we're just talking about the change. What do you think about it?

PAUL: Fine.

PEGGY: Just—fine?

PAUL: Yeah.

JUDY: Do you know about the budgets for this change, Paul?

PAUL: No.

JUDY: How about that new system they were talking about for combining Level One and Level Four deliveries?

PAUL: Which system?

JUDY: Weren't you at the meeting? End of the day yesterday?

PAUL: Oh, no. I left right at five. Had tickets to the game. Boy, the A's are playing well this year.

JUDY: The A's?

PEGGY: The A's. Baseball.

PAUL: Got stopped on the bridge going over, and Diane said we'd never get there, but we waited it out and pretty soon traffic broke up and we made it.

PEGGY: Who were they playing?

PAUL: Chicago.

JUDY: Paul, aren't you concerned about this change?

PAUL: Look, Judy, I've been here a long time. I've seen

a lot of changes. You just gut it out. Keep your head down and weather the storm.

PEGGY: Oh come on, Paul. When did you ever keep your head down? You're always right there, coming up with ideas.

PAUL: Well, yeah. Maybe so. But this is different.

JUDY: I agree. It *is* different. Just look what they're doing.

PEGGY: They're *doing* what needs to be done. Doesn't anybody see that? In six months, you won't even know this place.

JUDY: Yeah. If I'm still here in six months.

PEGGY: Oh come on, Judy; you know you'll be here.

JUDY: Well, maybe—

PEGGY: We just need to bite the bullet for a little while and everything will work out.

JUDY: Well, maybe you're right.

PEGGY: Don't you agree, Paul? We need to pitch in.

PAUL: Yeah. I guess you're right. What choice do we have?

In this interchange you see three different responses to the change. Judy's comments and questions are straightforward and informational. Still, there seems to be some underlying emotional issues as well.

- Confused—"I just need more information."
- Worried—"If I'm still here in six months."
- Uninformed—"How?" "When?"

Peggy, on the other hand, is very positive. She doesn't appear to have a problem, but it is possible that her positive attitude may pose a problem to others. In general, Peggy is:

- Positive—"It's great."
- Proactive—"I've been working this morning, fooling around with some ideas."

Finally, Paul is the hardest to read. The others see a change in him, but he is being tightlipped. Overall, Paul is:

- Removed—"I've been busy."
- Putting up a facade—"Fine." "Okay."
- Changing the subject—"Boy, the A's are playing well this year."
- Victim—"What choice do we have?"

At this point, place Judy, Peggy, and Paul on the Change Response Scale (Figures 5, 6, and 7).

Finally, take a look at Dennis who has come to talk to Rick.

FIGURE 5   How Judy Is Affected by Change

Judy:
Moving Away   0   2   4   6   8   10   Moving Toward
From Change   Change

FIGURE 6   How Peggy Is Affected by Change

Peggy:
Moving Away   0   2   4   6   8   10   Moving Toward
From Change   Change

FIGURE 7   How Paul Is Affected by Change

Paul:
Moving Away   0   2   4   6   8   10   Moving Toward
From Change   Change

DENNIS: Rick, hi. You got a sec?

RICK: Sure. Come on in.

DENNIS: Thanks. I realize with all the changes going on that time's probably a little precious right now.

RICK: Things are happening fast.

DENNIS: Yeah. They sure are.

RICK: Sit down.

DENNIS: Thanks. How are things going?

RICK: Pretty well. You know, we're moving along as fast as we can. How about yourself and the rest of the group?

DENNIS: Fine, fine. Just trying to keep going with what's happening now and thinking about the other things, but I sort of look forward to the prospect of some changes. It's sort of appealing.

RICK: I'm glad to hear you say that because I just found out something this morning and I wanted to get back to you as soon as possible. You, probably more than the folks in the immediate group, are going to be shifting and assuming some new responsibilities.

DENNIS: (After a pause) Such as?

RICK: With the phasing out of Level One and combining it with Level Four, you're probably going to be working with John's group more than you have before.

DENNIS: Does that mean I'm going to be taken out of creative?

RICK: No. No, you'll still be in creative. I wish I could be more specific about it right now. But I tell you what. Why don't you and John and I sit down and have lunch next week, and then we can talk about how these things are going to change. I should know more by next week.

DENNIS: Great. Well. It's all sort of a surprise, but it's interesting. I think I'm looking forward to it. That'll be good for me. I've always wanted to learn as much as I could, and this seems like a ripe opportunity for it. On the other hand, I honestly am going to miss working with those people. We've gotten a pretty tight bond. I feel real comfortable in that working relationship. There's some adapting I'm going to have to deal with.

RICK: It's going to be tough. But you're the kind of person who can make that shift. We've felt

that for a long time. And we appreciate having
somebody we know is going to be able to float,
change with the seasons, so to speak.

DENNIS: I'd appreciate it if you'd keep me up to date on
what's going on. I'll just take it and run if I can.

RICK: Will do.

DENNIS: Great. Thanks. Anything I can do, Rick.

RICK: Thanks.

In this scene you see Dennis deal with a change on top of a
change. Naturally, he has mixed emotions:

- Positive—"Looking forward to it . . ."
- Confused—"Will I still be in creative?"
- Lacking information—"How will it work?"
- Supportive—"Anything I can do."

Place Dennis on the Change Response Scale (Figure 8).

FIGURE 8   How Dennis Is Affected by Change

Dennis:

Moving Away	0 2 4 6 8 10	Moving Toward
From Change		Change

Now that you have looked at Rick and his team members
and how the change is affecting them, review your ratings for
each. You might like to compare your ratings with those most
commonly given:

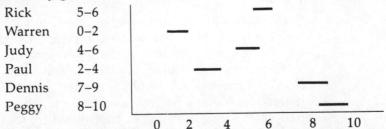

Rick	5–6
Warren	0–2
Judy	4–6
Paul	2–4
Dennis	7–9
Peggy	8–10

0   2   4   6   8   10

NOTE: Sometimes people give Dennis a 4, not believing that he
is intellectually supportive, but has emotional reservations.

As you can see, the reactions to the change range the entire
length of the scale which raises the questions, "So what? What
does all this information mean? Is it useful?"

USES OF THE CHANGE RESPONSE SCALE

An initial overview of how people are reacting to change is the essential first step in any intervention a manager or an employee plans to take. It provides a sense of how specific individuals are reacting, not how a group as a whole is reacting. It provides starting points and suggests strategies. It helps you to manage your own emotions.

Individual Reactions

When change occurs, people react differently. Repeating the analogy used earlier, they are tossed in the air and come down and land somewhere.

The cardinal rule in dealing with change is that where people come down is where they come down. Their reactions, whatever they are, are normal and natural for them given their experiences and the general circumstances.

It would be a serious error, then, to see the scale as evaluative, to see Warren's reactions as "bad" and Peggy's as "good." Unfortunately, this kind of judgment is exactly what happens all too often in changing environments. Anger or withdrawal is seen as *not* normal or natural; confusion is only tolerated. People are told their behavior is "inappropriate," that they have a "bad attitude," and that what management needs is flexible, proactive people willing to "rise to meet the challenge." This kind of rhetoric tells people, in effect, "What you are feeling is abnormal; something is wrong with you." As a result, the feelings go underground, the endings remain unaddressed, and the problems intensify.

Consequently, rule number one is that *position* on the Change Response Scale is *not* evaluative. It merely gives you a hypothesis of how people may be reacting.

Movement, on the other hand, *is* something which can be evaluated. The purpose of intervening in a change situation is to help start moving people *toward* ownership, gain, and resiliency. The operative word, then, is *movement*. Neither your intervention nor this book can be a pill to make people better quickly. Rather, the most effective type of intervention is recognizing where people are and then beginning a process of movement from endings through transitions to beginnings.

But how do you know that somebody whom you rate as a 6 is, in fact, a 6? The answer: Ask them. Some people have, in talking to others, said, "I see you as about a 4 on this scale. How do you see yourself?" This is not a secret rating system, but rather a common language people in change can use to get a sense of where others are. The most successful applications occur when work groups evaluate themselves in a two-step process.

Step One: An intact work group meets and everybody rates himself and everybody else individually. The scores are posted.

Step Two: Each individual then tells the group where he or she is on the scale and why.

The results of this exercise are enlightening. In most cases, the individuals rate themselves pretty much as the group did. In other cases, there are variances. In either case, the group has a chance to clarify issues, discuss differences, and make individual concerns and hopes known. One hears things like, "I didn't realize you felt that way. I'd have thought you felt just the opposite," and, "Now that I know that about you, maybe I can do something."

In addition to helping to show how other people are feeling, it is also often comforting to see that others are having problems too, when you may have been feeling like the Lone Ranger. Overall, the Change Response Scale is a simple tool to identify where people are and to help start the change process.

Strategies

If you are a manager or an employee, you can use the scale to help form a strategy for one-on-one communication. It tells you who is hurting the most and the least. It helps to externalize the issues.

Based on this information, you may set up a schedule for talking to people. If you were dealing with the Averco group, here are some possible strategies:

- Talk to Warren first; he is hurting the most.
- Do not talk to Warren first; come back to Warren when you are comfortable with the method.
- Talk to Judy first; a little bit of assurance and information will go a long way.
- Talk to Paul first; he is the "mystery" person; find out what is really bothering him.

As you can see, it is not *what* or *who* you choose that is the point. The point is that whatever you choose, you have chosen it based on the scale.

Self-Management

Often the response to seeing the completed scale is, "Hm. Things aren't as bad as I thought they were." Your estimation of a group's mood is almost always more negative than an objective evaluation of the individuals *in* that group. Thus without doing anything, a manager or employee can get an attitude boost just by seeing that things are not as bad as they seemed.

In general, any process that helps translate vague or rumor-laden information into clear information helps everybody involved. Even if the process surfaces new problems, at least you will know what they are and, therefore, be better able to address them.

Pre and Post

A final application for the Change Response Scale is ongoing measurement—ongoing temperature taking. The following story illustrates some of these uses.

A company went through a difficult series of changes. Things were difficult, but gradually got better. After six months the company seemed to be on the mend, and at one year the common wisdom was, "Everything's okay now." Still, there were production problems, rumors, and a sense of longing or regret.

In response to this situation, one group anonymously answered the following Change Response Scale:

1. Rate yourself as you felt one year ago.
2. Rate yourself now.
3. Draw an arrow indicating the direction you moved.

Their results are shown in Figure 9. Four employees moved forward; two remained at the same place; three moved backward. So much for "Everything's okay now."

FIGURE 9   The Change Response Scale Pre/Post

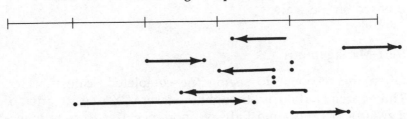

The basic reason given by those who moved forward was, "Promises and commitments were met"; for those who moved backward, "Promises and commitments were *not* met"; for those who remained the same, "Don't know yet."

This example underscores two important points to consider when working in a changing environment. First, people in change do not always go the way they're "supposed" to; monitoring is essential to insure that people do not get lost and fall through the cracks.

Second, this illustration explodes the myth that time heals all wounds—that given a year or so things will work themselves out on their own. In this company, endings were still unresolved, even a year after the initial trigger. They just were not as obvious or freely voiced as they had been at that time.

In general, the Change Response Scale is a simple, yet highly useful, tool in a changing environment. It is not an evaluation device, nor is it designed to be used "on" people; that is, it is not a secret scale for making judgments about people. It is best used as open information in existing work units. It is a shorthand method to enable people to declare themselves and to understand others.

5

ENDINGS: FOUR REACTIONS TO CHANGE

*Endings are, let's remember,
experiences of dying. They are
ordeals, and sometimes they
challenge so basically our sense
of who we are that we believe
they will be the end of us.*
William Bridges

You may remember the 1950s television program *Father Knows Best*. In one episode the father, Jim Anderson, comes home and announces that the family is moving. Even though they had discussed the move, the actual move causes markedly different reactions in the family members. Mrs. Anderson (Margaret) immediately inundates her husband with questions. Where? When? How? What about the kids' school? What about the mail? She is confused, anxious, and a little irritated. Jim's attempt to deal with her confusion by reminding her that they had discussed the matter does not lessen the intensity of her reaction.

The eldest daughter, Betty, a typical teenager with connections at school, freaks out. She will not hear of the move and, with the sentence she made famous, screams, "Oh, Father, how could you?" runs to her room, and slams the door. In contrast, Bud, the 14-year-old son, lounging on the couch in the living room, is more subdued. Feigning nonchalance, he answers his father's question, "You're okay with the move aren't you, Bud?" with, "Sure, Dad . . . that's fine . . . no problem." But he seems to be hiding his real feelings. Finally, Kathy, a grade schooler, is hurt by the announcement and fights back the tears. She has a part in the school play and feels she is being torn away.

Unlike the other family members, the father is, in *Aftershock* terminology, jumping to beginnings. He has already worked through the endings and transitions. So he tries to get everyone to jump to beginnings with him, but his attempt is totally inappropriate to where the rest of his family is.

What you see in the *Father Knows Best* scenario are four basic reactions to change. Some people are confused. Some people get angry. Some people withdraw; they pull back and will not let you know what they are feeling. And some people are very honestly worried or sad. Confusion, anger, with-drawal, and sadness/worry are the four key reactions. These are not abnormal reactions. On the contrary, they are what is to be expected. There is nothing wrong with reacting this way. If you *stay* in any one of these states for any length of time, however, then you are going to run into problems. But ini-tially, it is not a problem; it is a reaction.

This simple observation, that anger, confusion, sadness, and withdrawal are normal, runs counter to what many peo-ple experience during change. On the contrary, people who react in these ways are often told, "You shouldn't feel that way." "That attitude won't get you very far in this organiza-tion." As a result, people hide or deny their feelings. They repress the very feelings that could be the key to their suc-cessfully dealing with change. Admitting the feelings and facing them is the first step to recognizing that they must end.

In this chapter you will examine these basic reactions in more detail. You will look at both the negative and positive aspects of the reactions and how, by recognizing them, both in yourself and in others, you can begin moving from endings through transitions to beginnings.

The four reactions are the hub on which the skills and strategies turn. The names of the reactions are those used by William Bridges, although sometimes they are used in a little different sense than Bridges for the purpose of adapting them more directly to the issues of organizational change.

Four reactions to change are disengagement (withdrawal), disidentification (sadness/worry), disorientation (confusion), and disenchantment (anger).

DISENGAGEMENT

Val Margolis works in the operations department of a large bank. In response to recent declines in new customers and a realization that existing customers are not fully using many of

the bank's new services, management decided to take what
they termed "a more proactive approach" to educating and
attracting customers. Key to this process was the area of the
bank most familiar with these services—operations. "We need
you to be marketers," the operations people were told. "We
need to get you *and* your knowledge more squarely in front
of the customer."

The immediate effect of this decision was that the operations
department was reorganized and many people's jobs were
shifted, giving them more customer contact responsibilities. Val
was transferred from her old department and placed in a new
area. Now, more and more she is splitting her time between her
previous operations function and talking to bank customers on
the phone. She is working hard and performing adequately.
People who know her, however, have noticed that she is not the
"same old Val." She shows up for work, stays in her cubicle,
tends to avoid meeting the people in her new area, and leaves
right on time. When asked how she likes her new job, she says,
"Fine." She is very responsive to requests, but does not show the
kind of curiosity for which she was known in the past. At home
Val does not talk much about the change except to say that she
hopes there aren't any more. Her husband has noticed a sudden
increase in her attention to their garden.

At work, Val's new supervisor sees her as someone to count
on to get jobs done, but does not see the curiosity and inven-
tiveness that others say is so characteristic of her. As a result,
the supervisor no longer looks to her as someone to help give
identity to the new department.

Val is *disengaged.*

Bridges views disengagement as an actual physical removal, such as in the rites of passage in primitive societies. It
is equivalent to a divorce, a sudden physical impairment, or
the death of a loved one. It does little good to tell a person
experiencing this physical removal that it is probably "all for
the best," even though it may prove to be. By disengaging, you
become unattached from your society.

In the workplace, disengagement occurs when an individual reacts to the change issue by drawing back and appearing
to lose interest and initiative. It may be that individuals

perceive a negative outcome with implementing the change; therefore, they decide to do nothing and hope for the best. People experiencing disengagement may still put in their time at work, but do not put the energy or drive into their jobs that they once did. In general, disengaged people may be withdrawn.

On the other hand, they may *seem* to be engaged. They may say things like, "Fine, no problem. I'll do it." They may be upbeat and perky, but when you look beneath that perkiness you may ask yourself, "Am I getting commitment or am I just getting compliance?" Not all disengaged people are obviously withdrawn. They may protect themselves by pretending to be engaged.

Disengaged employees often mask their loss of commitment and adopt a "no problem" attitude. Behind this facade, however, are employees who have "quit and stayed."

The disengaged employee may quit or, more often, quit and stay.

You are probably familiar with the classic quit-and-stay, retired-in-place employee, the person who has been putting in his/her time for 20 years, punching the clock until retirement. That certainly is an example of being disengaged, but it is chronic, long-term disengagement. In a changing environment, you are more concerned with what you could call the *nouveau* disengaged person, somebody who was engaged yesterday but is not engaged today, who has had a real shift in behavior from commitment to compliance or from commitment to withdrawal. This sudden shift is an indication that the person has just recently disengaged, that he or she is reacting to change by drawing back.

Examples and typical responses of people who are disengaged include the following:

- They are the ones who quit and stay or "retire in place."
- They will "put in their time" but not give their energy.

- They often keep a low profile—possibly engage in passive/aggressive behavior.
- They may avoid talking about the change or change the subject.
- Their withdrawal is often an indication of a deeper fear or concern.

Typical behaviors include:

- Being hard to find.
- Doing only the basic requirements.
- Shrugging shoulders.
- Will not ask questions.
- Will not seek information.
- Will not discuss with others.

Typical verbal responses include:

- "Just keep your head down."
- "No problem."
- "It's okay."
- "I don't care."
- "What else is new?"
- "Anything you say."
- "I'll do my job."
- "No big deal."
- "It won't affect me."
- "It'll be temporary."
- "This happens every four or five years."

Disengagement is one of the most serious problems in organizations today. Unlike anger or worry or even confusion, which have outward signs, disengagement goes inward. The key to disengagement is the belief that if I endure, wait it out, it will change again, perhaps in my favor this time. So I will stick it out now as long as they continue to pay me. At a point in time when organizations need involvement, they are unwittingly fostering withdrawal. Management may pay lip service to employee creativity, telling them that in this era of

foreign competition and rising prices, they need people with new ideas, iconoclasts, risk takers. But by their insistence that people should feel good and be positive about change, they only drive the people who do not feel positive underground. They create a caste of people who have turned their personal energy into survival and self-absorption instead of into commitment to the organization and its new direction.

"Shields Up"

Earlier you learned that negative response to change was like drawing off energy; that is, the personal energy that would normally go into being productive is being rerouted into nonproductive behaviors. Each reaction to change, when it turns negative, draws off energy in its own particular way. With the disengaged person, energy that might otherwise go into adjusting to and moving with the change is shunted into insulation. Disengaged people use their energy to distance and insulate themselves from people and commitment, and from becoming involved in activity which, in their minds, will only bring more disappointment and setbacks. On the surface these people may seem listless and at low energy. But inside, they are expending great amounts of energy in avoidance.

The popularity in recent years of *Star Wars* and *Star Trek* space movies provides a good analogy for this behavior. The spaceships in these films generally have two main uses for their energy output: for space drive and for protective shields. When not at threat, the spaceships pour all their energy into their drive engines. But when they are attacked, the audience hears, in the words of Star Trek's Captain Kirk, "Red Alert. Shields up." Immediately the drive engines have to direct power to the shields, and if the energy in those shields is used up, the ship is helpless either to protect or drive itself.

When change hits, disengaged people do much the same thing. They pour energy into insulation—into their shields— fending off what they perceive as a threat from the organization and from others. As long as this energy is diverted into protection, these employees are unable to function at full strength. Rather, they take the path of least resistance, using up as little of their energy as possible for productive ends.

DISIDENTIFICATION

Don Prin used to service series 5000 machines, mostly copy machines, but now, as he puts it, "I don't know *what* I do." Don's company has recently moved him from California to the corporate headquarters in Colorado and assigned him to a team of technicians developing servicing techniques and procedures for the company's new line of copiers. It was a promotion. He was chosen because of his expertise and his excellent record. His new manager is expecting a lot from him.

Don says he is happy about the turn of events, but at some other level is a nagging sense that something is wrong. Both he and his boss have noticed it and pass it off as a result of the confusion surrounding suddenly moving his family from the Pacific to the Rockies.

At work, Don and a few of the other team members like to take time and reminisce about the days when they were white knights, how they would sometimes get calls in the night and would have to rush to panicked customers and resuscitate copy machines needed for vital jobs the next day. They were the experts, the company's front line. They could fix anything, and the inconvenience of occasional odd hours was more than offset by the customers' undying gratitude. "But now what are we?" Don and his colleagues joke. "Moles! Techies slaving away in the corporate basement."

Their humor and bravado have a definite edge to them. Throughout the day the conversation continually turns to war stories, complaints about their loss of a corporate car, and commiserating about the troubles their families are having adjusting to the move—new schools, house hunting, no babysitters, etc.

Moreover, their manager has noticed that Don does not seem to be catching on to the process of developing new servicing systems. He is beginning to take seriously Don's seemingly humorous contention that "I used to be an expert and now you've made me an incompetent." Specifically Don seems unable to distinguish between the *principles* of a servicing network and the *form* of the old network.

Don is *disidentified*.

Bridges suggests that a person experiencing disidentification has lost self-identification. Just as a lobster casts off its shell in order to grow, and for a brief period is soft and vulnerable, so disidentified individuals have lost their self-identity and are soft and vulnerable.

Disidentification occurs in change situations because something or someone that the individual identified with has been removed.

Typical things with which people identify strongly are specific tasks, a location, a work team, or a specific position. When one or more of these things are changed or taken away, there is a sense of loss not only of the job or the team, but also a loss of identity. These people's attachment to the past is strong because it gave them positive feedback, comfort, or a sense of belonging.

The telling phrase for disidentified people is, "I used to—" "I used to be a technical specialist. I used to be really good at my job. I used to work with a really good group of people. I used to really know my way around here."

These statements are usually accurate statements of fact. But they are only the first half of the full statement. It is the second half of the statement that causes the problem. For example, "I used to be a technical specialist, and now I'm nobody." "I used to be really good at my job, and now I'm incompetent." "I used to work with a really good group of people, and now nobody wants me." "I used to know my way around here, and now I'm lost."

In these classic disidentified statements, the clause before the comma is accurate; the clause after the comma is inaccurate, an exaggeration or a fear. To someone listening to these statements, they are clearly the result of the person jumping to unwarranted conclusions. To the person making the statement, it is perfectly true, but if you point out the inconsistency in the statement, declaring that "it's not true," the disidentified person may throw the first half in your face. "What do you mean? I am working with a different group aren't I?" This kind of irrational element is the hallmark of disidentification, a statement of fact followed by a nonsequitur catastrophized conclusion.

Disidentified employees usually have an attachment to a previous form, for example, the sales representative whose product line or territory has been changed, the employee who must be retrained, or the team whose members no longer work together. All these employees feel that "Since I used to be a this or a that (and am no longer), then what or who am I?" The disidentified employee feels stranded, like a fish out of water, and may feel frustrated and hurt, even betrayed.

Typical disidentified behavior includes:

- Reminiscing.
- Sulking.
- Dwelling on the past.
- Continuing to do the old job.
- Associating with the previous work team, at lunch for example, or after hours.
- Resisting new procedures, superiors, or tasks.

Typical verbal responses include:

- "It's not fair."
- "They didn't consult me."
- "It won't work."
- "I told you so."
- "Don't blame me if it doesn't work."
- "I'm washing my hands of it."
- "It was working fine, why change?"
- "My whole job is completely changed."
- "I used to—"

Disidentification, then, is much more than just sadness or worry. It is a frame of mind in which the irrational seems plausible. It is also a time of great vulnerability. Remember the lobster. It is true that the lobster must shed one shell so it can grow and develop another. It is also true that the lobster is, in fact, soft and vulnerable during this transition—a fact which could cost its life.

Similarly, during transition, the disidentified person is vulnerable and may, indeed, become the victim of his or her own self-fulfilling prophecy.

In the banking industry, for example, employees in operations jobs are being asked increasingly to become more like customer service representatives and "sell" some of the features of the bank. This change in roles plays havoc with the employees' sense of who they are. One man said, "I used to process loans, and now they want me to *sell* them—on the phone—to customers!" It is true that the employee in this case has been given certain customer contact responsibilities and has also been advised to advocate a particular type of loan if the options present themselves. In the man's mind, however, his job is now to sell. This is not true, of course. In reality, only a tenth of the job has changed, namely some customer contact responsibilities have been added. The employee's reaction, however, is that his identity has been changed, making him "incompetent," and the longer he believes that, the more likely it will become that his superiors will agree. And the employee will be replaced by someone else.

"Back to the Future"

The energy of disidentified employees, instead of going into productively adjusting and implementing the change, is going into the past. These people are focusing on a job or a location or a time that was stable and trying to live life as if that state of affairs had never changed.

The result of this intransigence is an unwillingness to adopt new methods and make new associations. Unlike the lobster, these employees want to return to the old shell and then, with that shell to protect them, try to move into the future.

DISORIENTATION

Sarah Lehmann made a deal with her boss, the director of new ventures at a midsized retail organization. "Be available and answer my questions," Sarah asked. "If you want me to head up this new Kiosk project, I'm going to need all the help I can get." Her boss's response was, "No question is dumb; no request too insignificant." Now, however, he is having second thoughts. Although he has not said anything, he has a sense that Sarah's questions are beginning to repeat themselves, and some of her requests, if not insignificant, are off the mark.

In the meantime, Sarah and her team are spending more and more time "clearing a space," as they put it. They have fallen significantly behind the timeline they set for project completion.

Sarah's project is one of several the company is trying out to regain some of the market share they lost due to competition. The Kiosk project is one of the most important new ventures because, if successful, it will put the company into shopping centers where they do not currently have retail stores. Sarah's response to being given the project was mixed. It was challenging, but it was definitely out of her area of expertise. For that reason, she made the deal with her boss to keep him available and responsive—so she could get up to speed.

Since then Sarah has deluged him with a never-ending flood of questions and requests. He responds, but that does not seem to do it for Sarah. Lately, she has been talking to other managers, trying to get a fix on how to begin. The more she inquires, it seems, the more there is to inquire *about*. Her people are waiting. "We're almost there," she tells them. "Just hang in there a little longer." Meanwhile, everybody is busy— "scurrying" as someone described it—but the direction is still not set. Sarah is concerned; her boss is concerned. The company is vulnerable, trying to regain their market share by trying new things. They are counting on Sarah and people like her to make this transition.

But Sarah is *disoriented*.

According to Bridges, disoriented employees are lost and confused. They do not know where they are or what they are feeling.

**Disorientation happens when an individual reacts
to the change situation by losing sight of
where he or she fits in.**

The disoriented employee expends energy trying to determine *what* to do instead of *how*. The past is this employee's only understanding of his or her responsibilities, priorities, and goals. Disoriented people tend to react very well to simple information—the more, the better. With this information, they can begin to make the bridge from the old to the new.

The organization that was, is no longer. And this person's reaction is, "I think I know what *I* am, but I'm not sure what the organization has become . . . so where do I fit in?" This person's reaction may express itself in the form of questioning, fear, or frustration. He or she cannot function fully or be "on purpose" until questions are answered.

Disorientation is characterized by:

- Confusion.
- Person has lost sight of where he or she fits in.

Typical behaviors of the disoriented employee include:

- Always asks questions.
- Does the wrong things.
- Gets others to ask questions.
- May worry unduly or even "catastrophize."
- Becomes very detail oriented.
- Involves others in questioning process.
- Does not know the priorities.
- Leaves work undone until questions are answered.

Typical verbal responses include:

- "Now what do I do?"
- "Now do I have to start all over?"
- "What do I need to learn?"
- "What's going on here?"
- "What do I do first?"

Disoriented employees are more than just confused. These people do not know the priorities or the direction of the department or company. Because they are not aware of the goals, their activity may be misdirected. They may be doing the wrong things, and if they were doing the right things, they would not necessarily know and could suddenly change and do something else. In general, the disoriented person is wandering, lost, and feeling left behind.

In many businesses today, disorientation is chronic. This problem can be understood by returning a moment to the Growth Curve presented in Chapter 2. When companies move from a normative to an integrative stage, their ability to set goals changes rather markedly. From the known, they are vaulted into the unknown. Therefore, the stable goals of the normative phase are replaced by risk taking and direction pointing. Clearly, the old style of management—here is the objective; here is the plan—is not fully possible in the integrative phase. Leadership, not management, is needed instead. Those in charge need to create visions and enlist people in fulfilling them rather than defining objectives and managing to their completion.

Employees who are accustomed to clear goals and direction will be easily disoriented if they expect the same kind of clarity in Phase III as was present in Phase II. This is not to say that clarity is not possible in the integrative stage. It is. It will just be different. It will tend to focus on short-term goals, steps, and a lot of communicating and monitoring. But if employees cannot get off their attachment to finite, long-term direction, and if management cannot deal with the ambiguity of moving targets, then disorientation will remain at high levels.

"Trivial Pursuit"

The energy of the disoriented person very often goes into scurrying or busy work. The mindset is, if you do not know what to do, at least do *something*. As a result, there is a lot of activity, a shotgun approach that reasons, "If I just try a lot of things, I'm bound to accomplish something."

Also, many disoriented people make a fetish of asking questions and gathering information. Their point of view might be one of being the guardian of what little sense of stability is left. So they go about gathering and consolidating, stipulating, in effect, the following condition, "I will put my energy into accepting and implementing the change, but *only* after I have *all* the information. In other words, you don't get my commitment *until* I get the information I demand." As a result, the energy output, and it may be great, is directed into attaining personal comfort rather than accomplishing organizational goals.

DISENCHANTMENT

Dave Enders is unhappy. He thought he was "safe" when the communications company he works for reorganized—and he *would* have been if they had not transferred him to a new office. Now he does not know what is going to happen. Dave's manager does not understand Dave's reaction. "This office is closer to your home," she reminds him, "and it's a newer office, a nicer work place. Not to mention that the job you've got now, even though it's a lateral move, has a lot more opportunity than your old one."

"Yeah, if it's still *here* in two months," Dave retorts.

This exchange is typical of Dave's behavior lately. His boss or other people explain the facts and benefits of his move, and he rebuts with an objection or sarcastic remark. People in the office ignored this behavior at first. They wrote it off as "normal adjustment." But now it is getting to be a problem. Dave is constantly on the "stump," putting down the company and encouraging others to do the same. And he has some takers. He seems to be the leader of a cadre of disgruntled people.

His manager has decided that this has got to stop. But she is reluctant to confront Dave about it, not knowing how he might react and afraid to find out. She also has noticed that his productivity has dropped off, and it seems as if he is purposely doing things to "prove" that the new system is unworkable, but she cannot be sure.

In all, she has a problem and the office has a problem because Dave is *disenchanted.*

Bridges describes this phase as when a person's world is no longer real. There is no Santa Claus. Some significant part of the individual's reality was in his or her head—for example, the perfect parent, spouse, child, leader, friend—and now it is gone.

**The disenchanted person realizes that
what is gone is gone.**

Instead of trying to repeat the past and find, as Bridges puts it, "a *real* friend, a *true* mate, and a *trustworthy* leader," this person is able to move on. The question is, "How quickly? How long will it take for the person to get over the blow and pick up the pieces? And what will that person be like in the meantime?"

In organizations, disenchanted individuals respond with anger to the change. They will eventually get over the disenchantment, but in the meantime will spend a great deal of time and energy communicating the negative. Attachment to the past is based on the employee's "victim" attitude, "Isn't it awful what they did to us?" Disenchanted people often try to enlist others in adopting their negative attitudes.

Their anger is almost always a smoke screen for one of the other three reactions to change. That is, once disenchanted employees have an opportunity to vent their anger, what emerges are feelings of disengagement, disorientation, or disidentification.

Characteristics of the disenchanted employee include:

- Outwardly displaying negativity; anger.
- Using anger to mask other problems.
- Enlisting support—"misery loves company."

Typical behaviors of a disenchanted employee include:

- Raised, intense tone of voice.
- Walks out.
- Refuses to talk.
- Shows self-pity.
- Tries to get others on his side.
- Backstabbing.
- Sabotage.

Typical verbal responses include:

- "It will never work."
- "I can't believe this is happening."
- "I'm getting out of here."
- "They'll be sorry."

Disenchantment in a changing environment is a difficult issue. On the one hand, it may not seem so bad. Again, although unpleasant, it is at least on the surface. Disenchanted people tend to get the issues out in the open. What makes it so problematic is that in a business environment, anger is "unacceptable behavior." Emotional displays in general and anger in particular are seen as childish and "unbusinesslike." As a result, disenchanted people often suppress their anger, and then it comes out in more insidious ways such as badmouthing, backstabbing, rumor-mongering, and even sabotage.

Some companies, fortunately, have a culture in which blowing your stack is okay. In those organizations, reaction tends not to be a large problem. But in a culture where it is taboo, otherwise forthright people find themselves masking and intensifying their reactions to change, thereby escalating rather than lessening the negative effects of that change.

"Blockage"

The energy of the disenchanted employee is more than just anger or passive/aggressive behavior. The energy is put into removing blockage. This blockage may be a resentment that the familiar is gone, that because no warning was given, the person can no longer trust people he or she once trusted, or a resentment that things that were once "true," such as a particular function, are no longer true. As Bridges points out, the profile for this type of person is to take some time, build up some steam, and then break through it and move on.

But what if the original blockage is being constantly increased—unwittingly—by a manager or a culture that is saying, "Don't act childish." "Take it or leave it." Or, "Oh, by the way, here's some more change." In these cases, the employee only increases the force of energy put against the ever-mounting blockage.

The result can be serious, because anger unbridled can lead to extreme personal problems and overtly destructive behavior. The literature is filled with stories of innocent victims of injustice who, when they seek redress, do not get it and eventually transform themselves into insufferable tyrants. This type of character and story is the prototype of the disenchanted person. Ironically, the problem that may be the easiest to deal with turns out in the end to have the greatest and longest-lasting ill effects.

BIG "D," LITTLE "d"

To this point the problems associated with the four reactions to change have been stressed. These reactions are not necessarily negative, however. On the contrary, as noted, they are normal, human reactions to a change or a stress stimulus. Everyone has them, and in any given situation, virtually everybody involved will react in one or more of these ways. Even someone who is very positive about the change could easily be somewhat disoriented or perhaps a little disidentified. That person's sense of gain rather than loss, however, tends to enable him to turn his reaction more quickly into an ownership response to the changing situation.

These reactions are also natural coping mechanisms to deal with sudden shifts. As one person put it, "When I get hit with change, I tend to disengage, that is, pull back, be reflective, maybe even hold people at bay for a while—long enough for me to figure out what happened and get my bearings. During these times people say they can't read me, and I guess they can't. But I find this disengagement very beneficial and helpful, and I don't intend to stop it. It's the one thing I've found that really helps me." Later on this person added, "But if I *stay* disengaged, that's another matter. *Then* it's a problem."

This statement succinctly outlines the issue of the change reactions. They begin as natural and normal responses—healthy and potentially productive. But if extended, if the person cannot move through the reaction, then it becomes a problem. Examples of such reactions follow.

It is essential to recognize not only the down-side, but also the up-side of these reactions.

Disorientation. Confusion and a desire for direction certainly have positive elements. They enable people to clarify key questions, get answers, seek out information, and formulate plans and ideas. Disoriented people are very likely to be those who get to the key issues or who flush out problems that could arise later.

Disidentification.   A sense of the past is very important in a changing environment. Since some, but not all, of what exists will change, there needs to be someone with a sense of what is valuable in the existing structure and a sense of how it can be transferred or adapted to the new. Such a person prevents the proverbial baby from being thrown out with the bath water.

Disengagement.   Reflection is a valuable skill. Indeed, the thesis of this book advocates *not* jumping to beginnings but pulling back long enough to evaluate the situation. Disengagement is also valuable for personal reasons. A mental breather or break, a time to collect thoughts, is a key self-management skill in a change situation.

Disenchantment.   Anger has its place. Certainly it gets the issues out. Also, allowed to vent, people tend to feel better; they have been allowed, in effect, to expel the blockage and feel a good deal better for it. However uncomfortable some people may be with raised voices or intense discussions, no one can deny the value in getting things into the open. As the disengagement advocate mentioned earlier put it, "I'd much rather deal with someone who is angry than someone like me."

The question you might ask yourself is this, "Is my response to change a reaction (small "d") or is it a problem (large "D")? Am I having feelings of disidentification, being cut off from things I valued, or am I *disidentified*, irrationally longing for what used to be and, therefore, not dealing well with change?"

You might want to evaluate yourself in terms of your current reaction to change. Take a few minutes to complete, either with a pen or mentally, the following questions:

1. Think about a change you are going through now at work. Pretend you are a camera. You have been videotaping yourself for the last week or two. What is on the videotape? What do you see? What do you hear?

2. If *someone else* saw this videotape, would that person say you were disidentified, disenchanted, disoriented, and/or disengaged? Explain.

3. How do *you* feel about the change and what is happening for you?
4. Do you feel disidentified, disenchanted, disoriented, and/ or disengaged? Explain.

By looking at your reaction from the "camera's" as well as your own point of view, it is possible to get insights into your own behavior. In this process you may identify one or several reactions you have having. Perhaps you are having different reactions to different changes. You may also be a little "d" or big "D."

Whatever the case, you have given yourself some information. You have begun to answer the first half of the endings question, "How does change affect me and the people I work with?" The answer to that question, whether a little "d" or a big "D," is your starting point. In later chapters you will learn the next step, dealing with your reactions and those of others.

IN SUMMARY

The four reactions to change are:

DISENGAGEMENT
"Quit and stay."

DISIDENTIFICATION
"I used to be somebody."

DISORIENTATION
"Where do I fit in?"

DISENCHANTMENT
"Ain't it awful!?"

Although by no means a mutually exclusive and finite set of definitions, these four distinctions provide a simple, useful tool for identifying and describing some behaviors that will help answer how change affects people. You can diagnose the reactions to change by observing behavior and listening to verbal and nonverbal communication.

Once these distinctions are made, you will have a working diagnosis. You will have a sense of what others may be experiencing, and, therefore, you will have taken the first step in effectively dealing with the reaction.

Finally, it is important to understand that people can have more than one reaction to change. You may have a co-worker who is both disoriented and disengaged. Generally, however, people tend to gravitate to one of the four reactions. This may vary from change to change, but at any given time, people tend to exhibit one of these reactions more than another.

THE REACTIONS TO CHANGE AT AVERCO

In the last chapter you placed some Averco employees on the Change Response Scale. Now that you have a better understanding of the four reactions associated with change, return to the Averco Corporation and try to determine what reactions and/or problems the employees may be exhibiting. The scene takes place in the Averco lunchroom where Peggy, Warren, Judy, and Paul are discussing the week that is winding up. As you follow along with their conversation, underline or at least note specific phrases indicative of a reaction to change: disengagement, disidentification, disorientation, or disenchantment.

PEGGY: Boy, what a week this has been! I have never worked so hard in my entire life. But you know, I am really excited about all these changes that are coming in.

WARREN: You mean you really get excited about making fruitless efforts?

PEGGY: Now, Warren, you can't deny that we've needed to implement these changes to put this company on the leading edge.

WARREN: We have *been* on the leading edge. I mean, we've worked very hard to put us *on* the leading edge. Now is not the time to—

JUDY: Change?

WARREN: Change for change's sake is pointless. It's a deadend street. Can't you see that, Peg?

PEGGY: Warren, if you had your way we'd be back with buggies. Now come on. This is exactly what we need to do to start moving ahead.

WARREN: What? The company's position, huh? Do you have a place on the Executive Committee now? A new V.P. here?

PEGGY: What do you think, Paul? How do you feel about all these changes?

PAUL: I don't know. I've seen a lot of changes. Some of them work out. Some don't.

JUDY: Do you know what you're aiming for? What about budget? Have you talked to Rick about budget changes?

PEGGY: No. But I have a meeting with Rick. There are a lot of things I don't know. I'm planning to discuss a lot of things with him. Hopefully, he can clear them up.

JUDY: Do you know what you're going to do in your department, Paul?

PAUL: No.

Enter Dennis.

DENNIS: Hi, everybody.

PEGGY: Hi. How've you been?

DENNIS: Busy. Real busy. Besides all the changes in general that have gone on around here, I'm going through some additional changes. I just found out from Rick that I'm going to be working under John.

PEGGY: That's great!

DENNIS: Yeah, I guess so—I mean, I think it is, but it's sort of a surprise. Since they're grouping One and Four together now, they're going to be putting me into some different areas.

JUDY: Are you still going to be in creative?

DENNIS: Yeah, at least for right now I am. I'm not sure about the details. Rick's going to get back to me. But for now I am.

WARREN: So now they're going to just start moving everybody around. It's crazy. I've got people counting on me, and I don't know what to tell them. I used to be able to help, but now I'm worthless.

DENNIS: Warren, all I can say is what Rick told me. I'm going to be doing some floating back and forth. As far as I know the group's going to stay together. I'm going to be working with the group for a while myself, but that's down the road. I don't know.

JUDY: What about the old creative department? Now that we're combining, who's going to be in charge?

DENNIS: I'm not really sure. I'll be reporting to John, but that's all the detail I know.

JUDY: I wish I knew how this was going to work out. Until then, our hands are tied.

WARREN: You're telling me! Is this just the beginning? I mean is everyone going to be moved around?

DENNIS: I'm really not sure what's going to happen. All I know is I'm going to be floating back and forth in some different areas. As far as the rest of the group goes, I'm not sure.

WARREN: I can tell you. What we're seeing here is the beginning of the end. Isn't that right, Paul?

PAUL: Could be.

DENNIS: What do you think, Paul? I mean, you've been here for a while. What do you foresee?

PAUL: Look. I'm not affected by this. I'm just going to keep doing my job and weather the storm.

Based on what you observed in the preceding scenario and given the four reactions to change and their potential for problems, you can begin to identify the reactions of the Averco employees.

Judy appears to be Disoriented (big "D"). She is constantly asking questions, seems confused, and feels until she knows fully what is going on, her "hands are tied."

Warren is clearly and strongly Disenchanted. Dennis' announcement of more change only increased the blockage and, therefore, escalated Warren's anger. He is also apparently Disidentified. His statement, "I used to be able to help, but now I'm worthless," is a classic disidentified statement in which a true first clause is followed by an exaggerated or irrational second clause. His disorientation probably runs deeper, but is being overshadowed by his anger.

Dennis seems to be doing pretty well, although there seems to be a little disorientation in his reaction, which is fully understandable under the circumstances. Also, there may be a little disengagement as he tries to sort out what is going to happen to him. Generally, however, he seems to be looking forward to the change. He just wants some clarity.

Peggy is very positive and has either chosen or been put in the position of "cheerleader." As a result, it is hard to see much of a reaction other than some mild disorientation about goals and procedures. She has probably worked through her reactions, however, and is already into a beginning. This is good news in one sense but a potential problem in another. Her positive attitude tends to be an irritant to some of the others. She appears to want them to jump to where she is.

Paul is clearly and classically Disengaged—so withdrawn that it is impossible to tell what he is really thinking or feeling. The only rise the group was able to get out of him was when they pressed him and he asserted, "Look, I'm not affected by this," telling them, in effect, to mind their own business and leave him alone.

Rick was not at the table, but based on what you saw and heard in previous chapters, it is fair to say that he is Disoriented and perhaps also manifesting a little disenchantment. The Disorientation results from his not really knowing what is going on and getting pressure from both his boss and his people. His disenchantment is more irritation than anger.

Looking at all the people in the department, you see big "D" problems and little "d" reactions. Whether they are reactions or problems is not the key point, however. As mentioned in the discussion of the Change Response Scale, where people are is where they are. The main point is to look at all of them in terms of what needs to be overcome or worked through and what each has to offer. The following chart gives a partial picture of this breakdown:

Person	To Overcome	To Offer
Warren	Anger	Energy and expertise
Judy	Hang back/question	Detailed knowledge
Paul	Withdrawal	Do not know
Dennis	Doubt/confusion	Willingness to try new things
Peggy	"Cheerleader" pose	Energy, enthusiasm
Rick	Confusion	Leadership/concern for others

The following chapters concern themselves with overcoming the problems and capitalizing on the strengths.

6

THE SELF-MANAGEMENT PROCESS

Know thyself.
Socrates

I was telling myself all sorts of awful things, and what's worse, I believed me.

When change occurs, people react. Their reaction may cause them problems, or it may start them on their way, moving through endings and transitions to beginnings. This process is natural, and even for people who hang on to their endings for a long time, there is eventual movement. The purpose of this book, as noted, is not to circumvent or skip stages in this process but to help speed it up, specifically to develop skills to help move yourself and others toward beginnings. In this and the next two chapters, you will be introduced to the skills for fostering this movement.

Ideally, it would be nice if somebody else would make the effort to help you deal with changes. Wishing for this kind of help is, in one sense, a natural desire, but in another sense, it is the reverse of the victim mentality "they" did it to me; now "they" had better undo it. In some instances what starts as a natural request for some assistance gradually becomes a demand. People say, in effect, "You owe it to me."

But what if nobody helps you deal with change? Is there anything you can do on your own to help yourself? This chapter addresses that question and provides a self-management technique to help you sort out your own responses to change and move forward. To begin this process, recall the Averco employees, Warren, Rick, Peggy, Paul, Judy, and Dennis, and their varying degrees of disidentification, disenchantment, disorientation, and disengagement. Also, recall your own response to the exercise asking you to identify your own reactions. The question underlying all of these responses is, "How did *they* and how did *you* get that way in the first place?" That question is the starting point for self-management.

SELF-TALK

Do you talk to yourself? If you ask a group of people that question, about three-quarters or so will raise their hands. The logical next question is, "Can we assume that those of you who didn't raise your hands are saying to yourself, 'I don't talk to myself?'"

We all talk to ourselves. In fact, no matter what we are doing, we almost always have a running conversation with ourselves. The question is, "What are you telling yourself? And what effect, if any, is that conversation having on you?" Take the last question first. "What is the effect of self-talk?"

Ask yourself, "Are you careful what you say to other people?" The answer is probably yes. You watch what you say to others because what you say can influence them positively or negatively. You do not want to offend people or hurt their feelings. You do not want to be misunderstood, so you are careful.

Now ask yourself, "Are you as careful about what you say to yourself as you are about what you say to others?" The answer is probably no!

You say things to yourself that you would *never* say to others. For example, "This will never work," or "You idiot." In general, people are prone to say all sorts of denigrating things to themselves which, if they said them aloud to other people, would have a decidedly negative effect. "But I know me," you might protest. "I know I'm just kidding." Perhaps. But on the other hand, you may underestimate the cumulative effects that your own self-talk can have on you. The term *self-fulfilling prophecy* is just one expression of a generally recognized tendency for people to, in effect, sometimes be their own worst enemies.

Assuming, then, that you can work against your own best interests by what you say to yourself, return to the first of the two questions. "What are you telling yourself? What, exactly, are you saying to yourself that is having ill effects?"

This question is much more difficult to answer because the term "self-talk" is a generic term for a host of things, including thoughts, feelings, attitudes, reactions, and experiences. Consequently, to present in simple verbal form the combination of elements that constitute self-talk would be impossible.

For that reason, at this point you will depart from a psychological discussion of those things that go under the name self-talk and, instead, look at some dramatizations of self-talk to get a sense of its effects.

The convention used is one you are probably familiar with, from the cartoon strip *Peanuts*, by Charles Schultz. In that strip, one of the standard items is Lucy's psychology stand. The recipient of Lucy's services is generally Charlie Brown, and as a rule when he goes to Lucy, he gets only one kind of advice—bad advice.

Negative self-talk is like Lucy's advice. In effect, all of us go to our own Lucys, engage in self-defeating conversations, and give ourselves bad advice.

As you may remember, the Averco employees, Warren, Judy, Paul, and Rick, all had various problematic reactions to change: Warren was disenchanted and disidentified; Judy was disoriented; Paul was disengaged; and Rick was disoriented and disenchanted. The question now is, "How did they get that way?"

If you asked them, they would undoubtedly say, "The change made me that way." True, the change was the trigger event, but to what extent did they have a part in the process? To what extent did they create their own problems?

To dramatize their cases, picture Lucy's psychology stand.

Warren

The first patient to approach the stand is Warren. And behind the stand sits Warren. Thus Warren is talking to himself; Warren the *"Doctor"* is talking to "Warren" the person.

WARREN: Look, I've got a problem.

DOCTOR: (Vaguely bored) That's what I'm here for.

WARREN: We just had a big change in our company.

DOCTOR: (Suddenly attentive, interrupts) A change?! Oh, great!

WARREN: Yes, something wrong?

DOCTOR: Wrong? Are you kidding? A change? That's terrible.

WARREN: Change is terrible?

DOCTOR: (Mimicking Warren) Change is terrible? (Forcefully) Of *course* it's terrible. What planet are *you* from? (Pause—Wearily) Okay, okay, give it to me. What are they doing to you?

WARREN: Well, they're phasing out Level One and integrating it with Level Four.

DOCTOR: Oh, is *that* all? Out with One, in with Four. And, don't tell me, you're in Level One, right?

WARREN: Basically, yes.

DOCTOR: Yes! he says. And you're probably an expert, right?

WARREN: Yeah.

DOCTOR: *The* expert. I knew it.

WARREN: Well, not exactly. But I did—

DOCTOR: (Interrupting) But nothing. (Pause) You *were* the expert. So let me ask you this. What are you now? Huh?

WARREN: Well—

DOCTOR: (Interrupting) You're *nothing!* That's what you are!

WARREN: Nothing?

DOCTOR: Nada. (Pause) I can see it now. People are going to come up to you—the expert—check that—ex-*ex*pert. And they're gonna want answers. And guess what, buddy?

WARREN: Well, I—

DOCTOR: You're not gonna have 'em. That's what.

WARREN: I won't be the expert?

DOCTOR: Ha! Are you kidding?

WARREN: So, you're saying people will come to me—

DOCTOR: Yes!

WARREN: And I won't be able to answer their questions?

DOCTOR: No way. You're not gonna know didley.

WARREN: I used to be somebody.

DOCTOR: But not anymore. Now, you're done for!

WARREN: (Rising anger) Hey, wait a minute. They can't do this to me!

DOCTOR: Now you're getting the spirit.

WARREN: It's not fair. It's—stupid, dumb.

DOCTOR: (Motioning with hands) Keep talking. Keep talking.

WARREN: I'm not going to take it!

DOCTOR: That's it! Fight 'em! That's your only out.

WARREN: You bet I will. I won't stand for this.

DOCTOR: You go get 'em.

WARREN: I will. Thank you. (Warren leaves, quickly returns, reaches into his pocket, pulls out a nickel, and puts it on the counter) They're gonna be sorry they did this to me.

DOCTOR: (Smiling smugly) Right on! Give it to them. They deserve it.

In the process of talking to himself, Warren goes from stating facts to rabblerousing. He starts off simply mentioning that he is up against a problem—a change—at which point the "Doctor" shoots back the kneejerk response, "That's terrible." From that point onward, facts are used only to support the "Doctor's" ongoing catastrophizing.

In effect, Warren talks himself into being a victim. The only proactive measure he plans to take now is to fight. With the same beginning, he could have just as easily started looking for solutions and measures to deal positively with the change. But by believing—not questioning—the initial reactive thought and letting it control his thinking, the result, as you saw earlier, was his loud confrontation with Rick.

Judy

Next consider Judy as she goes somewhat hesitantly to the psychologist's stand to get her nickel's worth of advice.

JUDY: Hello?

DOCTOR: Yes. How may I help you?

JUDY: Well, we've just had a change and reorganiza-
          tion at our company.

DOCTOR: Oh, my.

JUDY: Yes—and I was wondering if you could give
          me some advice on how to handle it?

DOCTOR: Yes, certainly. I'll just take a few notes if you
          don't mind. Now, to begin, how extensively is
          your area affected?

JUDY: *Very* extensively. There'll be new procedures,
          products, staff changes—plus unknowns.

DOCTOR: Oh, dear. And will you be able to predict the
          course of the changes—so far as they affect
          you?

JUDY: No.

DOCTOR: I see. That's quite serious. But, the current sys-
          tem you have, is it an effective one?

JUDY: Oh, yes, very much so.

DOCTOR: I see, I see.

JUDY: Do you—have any suggestions—advice—
          maybe?

DOCTOR: Well, one can never be sure in these cases—
          but yes, I think there are some things you
          might consider.

JUDY: Like?

DOCTOR: Well, to begin, I recommend that you not let
          go of your present procedures *until* the new
          procedures are fully explained and their im-
          plementation fully integrated.

JUDY: I'm not sure that's entirely possible. You see,
          there's—

DOCTOR: (Miffed) Well, of course, the choice is yours.
          But you can't very well let go of one system
          until there's another to take its place, now can
          you?

JUDY: Well—

DOCTOR: Not unless you want to risk being caught
          without a system.

JUDY: Yes, I see—

DOCTOR: (Adding quickly) By the way, have you kept your resume' up to date?

JUDY: Actually, no, not as much as—

DOCTOR: (Cutting in) So then you don't really have a choice, do you?

JUDY: (Pensive, worried) Hmmmmmmmmmm.

DOCTOR: But I paint a grim picture, don't I? Actually, perhaps your best strategy is to gather information before acting or committing to anything.

JUDY: (Brightening) Yes, that would be comfortable to me.

DOCTOR: Be proactive, mind you. Diligent. But do *not*, under any circumstances, change to the new system—

JUDY: (Finishing the thought) Until I have adequate information and assurances regarding the new system's operation and implementation.

DOCTOR: (Delighted) Yes, exactly. (Politely sarcastic) If they *can* provide such information and assurances. (Laughs) The possibility of which, frankly, I have my doubts.

JUDY: (Not sure if she agrees) Yes. (More directly) But I should keep busy?

DOCTOR: Oh, by all means—and *committed* as well. (Slyly) *Out*wardly at least. But don't commit to the change until *all* of your questions are answered—

JUDY: *All* of them?

DOCTOR: *All* of them. Now isn't that splendid advice?

JUDY: (Self-absorbed, not sure she agrees—Part of her says "yes," part says "no") Well, yes, I suppose it is. Thank you.

DOCTOR: Not at all. Have a nice day.

Unlike Warren, Judy is very calm and very logical with herself. She takes time to consider the facts, weighs the comfort of the old system against the ambiguity of the new one, and convinces herself not to commit to a course of action, but rather to one of inaction—of not committing to the new system until "all" of her questions are answered. This, she concludes, is comfortable.

More cautious than Warren, Judy also covers her tracks. She decides to look outwardly committed and busy, but inwardly rigid. Thus Judy moves on the Change Response Scale away from resilience toward rigidity. As an ongoing motivation, Judy also sets the seed in her own mind that since she has no immediate prospects for other employment, she really "has no choice" in the matter. Convinced that there is no net to catch her and no other trapeze readily at hand, she clings to her old trapeze, even though its ropes are fraying.

The only positive note in the conversation is Judy's final answer to the "Doctor's" question, "Now isn't that splendid advice?"

"Well," Judy says, somewhat unsurely. "Yes, I suppose it is."

This conversation and her parting reluctance manifested itself in her conversation with Peggy and Paul and in her conversation at lunch. She is groping, questioning, unsure whether to pull back or to move out a little and take some positive action. Her reaction is not as problematic as Warren's, but she is still hamstrung by her ambivalence and disorientation.

Paul

It's now Paul's turn to visit the psychologist's booth to consult the "Doctor." Paul approaches very tentatively and sits down as the Doctor is busy writing.

DOCTOR: (Looking up) Oh, hi.
PAUL: H'lo.

Uncomfortable pause.

DOCTOR: Can I help you?
PAUL: Me? Nah. I'm fine.
DOCTOR: They why are you—

PAUL: Here? Oh, just saw that you were "in."

DOCTOR: In? (Looks at sign) Oh, yes, so I am. (Another uncomfortable pause) Soooooo. What's been happening?

PAUL: Oh, nothing really. Just a change situation over at work.

DOCTOR: A change, eh. Big one?

PAUL: Naw. Just a change. You know how it is. They're always changing in my business.

DOCTOR: Sure, I know what you mean. (Weak laugh) Change is the only constant, right?

PAUL: Right. Right. (Trying to be nonchalant) It affects some of the other people—

DOCTOR: But not you.

PAUL: Me? Naw. I just keep my head down. Weather the storm. But some of those others. Well, they feel bad about, you know, the way we used to do things, teamwork, things like that.

DOCTOR: Yeah. It's sad when people feel that way. (Changes subject) You don't follow baseball, do you?

PAUL: A little. Why do you ask?

DOCTOR: Oh, I don't know. Just curious.

PAUL: Um hm. (Lapses back to his concern; this time a little more forcefully) Especially teamwork.

DOCTOR: Beg your pardon?

PAUL: Teamwork. I mean we really used to work together, cross-fertilize ideas, help each other out. And with this new system, we're not doing that. And that's what we need—*really* need right now.

DOCTOR: D'you say something?

PAUL: (Almost says "yes") No. I was just thinking about—

DOCTOR: Those other people.

PAUL: Yeah, those other people.

DOCTOR: So. You seem to be handling this change pretty well.

PAUL: Yeah. I guess you could say that.

DOCTOR: Keeping busy I take it?

PAUL: Oh, hey. I put in my eight hours.

DOCTOR: Work hard.

PAUL: Like I always have.

DOCTOR: That's what I like to hear. And you know what you might want to do?

PAUL: What's that?

DOCTOR: (Lowering his voice) You might want to—well—maybe keep your distance from the others for a while. What with them getting all upset, excited, you know, just until this thing blows over.

PAUL: Yeah, I think you may be right.

DOCTOR: Of course I'm right.

PAUL: Yeah. That's what I'm going to do.

In this scene, and for the first time, you finally discover what Paul has been harboring, namely a sense of loss regarding the "team." Paul has been with the company from the beginning. Given this fact, you can assume that he values the team spirit that probably existed in the company's formative stage. Whether that sense of teamwork has endured up until just before the change is unimportant. What *is* important is that Paul thinks so. Thus the change is the final straw, and his sense of loss is acute.

Instead of verbalizing that loss, however, Paul has withdrawn into himself—a process that this scene makes painfully apparent. Paul is a house divided. One part of him wants to talk about the sense of teamwork, but the other part of him wants to avoid it. Consequently, Paul and his "Doctor" dance around the issue, with the "Doctor's" point of view winning out. Paul convinces himself that if he just lies low until the whole thing "blows over," maybe things will be like they were.

THE EFFECTS OF NEGATIVE SELF-TALK

In these scenes you have been able to trace, in a dramatized form, the result of negative self-talk and its effects. Warren talked himself into a victim mentality resulting in disenchantment and disidentification. Judy subtly moved toward rigidity and disorientation. And Paul, before he really knew it, had backed himself into an overwhelming sense of loss and disengagement.

Rick

Like the others, Rick, too, goes to his "Doctor" to get his own special brand of bad advice. Before you eavesdrop on that conversation, however, it is necessary to broaden the context.

About a week after the initial announcement, Rick and his boss, Carter, have the following conversation:

RICK: So, Carter, I think I have my thoughts a lot better organized than I did at the meeting last week, and I think I know where we're going with this.

CARTER: Good.

RICK: I've had a chance to get around to my people in the last couple of days and talk to them about how they're feeling about this. There are some concerns everyone has. Basically everyone's concerned about how each section is going to handle budget, staffing, and work flow problems. But there's a limit to what we can do until we know the priorities of . . .

CARTER: Rick, I get the feeling you don't think we're doing anything about this. We're working on a staff transition team and a placement transition team. We might even have to get into new real estate to handle some of these new configurations.

RICK: Good. You're talking about space arrangements. I mean everybody's wondering about that. Who's going to be working with whom and where—

CARTER: Rick, I can't answer those questions right now.
          I can't *give* you those specifics. You're just go-
          ing to have to handle your people, do your job.
          Let me get my ducks in a row, okay? Then
          I'll come to you and we'll solve some of your
          larger corporate problems. I can't do that now.

RICK: Carter, you know we're working under a very
          tight time-frame here.

CARTER: Don't talk to me about the time frame. I *know*
          about the time frame. (Pause) Rick, look, we're
          under a lot of tension. All of us. You're a good
          manager. One of my best. I've got to do my job.
          You've got to do yours. I'm counting on you.

Rick has a dilemma. On the one hand, he is tense because
he does not know what is going on and is being pressured by
his people. On the other hand, he is getting pressure, but no
support from Carter. Carter says a lot of nice things about
Rick, "You're a good manager," and so on, but all these plati-
tudes do not help because they do not address real problems.
Even if he sincerely means them, they did not have any tactical value. They are at best just a compliment, at worst a way of
writing him off.

Rick is feeling the squeeze. He has his people asking him
lots of questions, saying in effect, "I won't work until you give
me this or tell me that," and he has Carter not giving him the
information he needs, but expecting results.

One way of graphically representing Rick's dilemma is by
using the Management Rectangle.

THE MANAGEMENT RECTANGLE

Ideally, the three major areas—the department, the manager,
and the organization—are equally balanced, as in Figure 1.
In this system, everyone is pulling his or her own weight,
sharing the load.

If Rick were to draw the rectangle to represent his situation,
however, he would probably draw it as shown in Figure 2.

Rick may perceive the organization taking up two-thirds
of the rectangle, his employees taking up one-quarter of the

FIGURE 1   FIGURE 2

| organization |
| manager |
| department |

| organization |
| manager |
| department |

diagram, and him taking up the remainder. In effect, the corporation is "coming down" on them. A manager in this situation feels "squeezed." The organization is controlling change here, imposing change on the manager, pressing him. When this is true, the employee's perception of management is that it is simply a voice of the organization.

Rick is also getting pressure from his employees. They are asking, demanding answers and action. In organizations where employee pressure is greater than organization pressure, the rectangle might look as illustrated in Figure 3.

In this situation, the employees usually perceive such managers as representing them. Although managers in this rectangle are popular with their employees, they are not achieving company objectives.

Rick, however, is getting pressure from both ends. So, in the final analysis, Rick's rectangle probably looks as shown in Figure 4. Taking this pressure out to its logical conclusion, you would get the situation illustrated in Figure 5.

FIGURE 3   FIGURE 4

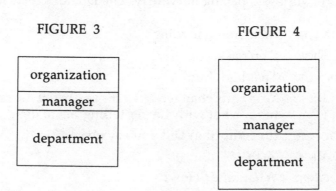

| organization |
| manager |
| department |

| organization |
| manager |
| department |

FIGURE 5

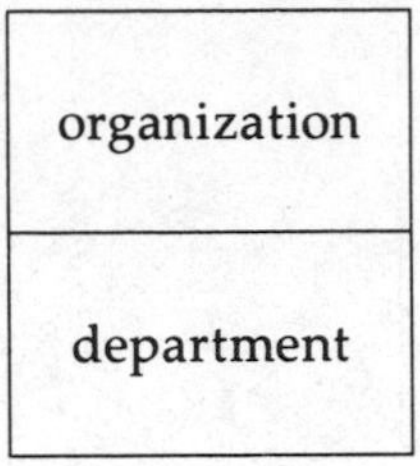

```
┌─────────────────────┐
│                     │
│    organization     │
│                     │
├─────────────────────┤
│                     │
│    department       │
│                     │
└─────────────────────┘
```

In this management rectangle the manager is *missing*. This illustrates a situation in which employees perceive that they cannot find their manager when they need to, and the organization perceives the manager as ineffective. This management rectangle illustrates what is known as the *transparent manager*. The various configurations the management rectangle might take are illustrated in Figure 6.

Of most serious consequence is the transparent manager. If managers decide not to deal with the changes and remove themselves from the managing role or simply acquiesce to mandates, they communicate a strong negative message to their employees. They become the ultimate victims, and they might very likely get caught up in their own negative self-talk.

Rick

Picture Rick coming up to the psychiatrist's stand, a little flustered, uptight, pacing nervously. The Doctor greets him.

DOCTOR: Rick, how's it going?

RICK: Don't ask.

DOCTOR: That bad, huh?

RICK: Yeah, this change. . . . It's really got me running, what with Carter telling me to do . . .

DOCTOR: (Interrupting) Did you say change?

RICK: Yeah.

DOCTOR: What kind? How?

FIGURE 6   The Management Rectangle

<table>
<tr><td>
organization

manager

department
</td><td>
organization

manager

department
</td></tr>
</table>

Manager feels imposed upon by the organization. Employees see manager as a "voice of the organization."

Manager perceives self as a victim.

Manager feels imposed upon by the employees. Manager is popular with the department but is not achieving company objectives.

Manager perceives self as a victim.

<table>
<tr><td>
organization

department
</td><td>
organization

manager

department
</td></tr>
</table>

Manager is "transparent." The "transparent manager" ignores the change and removes self from the employees and the organization.

The "transparent manager" is the ultimate victim.

Manager becomes an active manager of the change rather than a passive bystander. You manage how much of the rectangle you occupy.

Manager perceives self as an owner of the change.

RICK: Reorganization. Level One out; Level Four in.

DOCTOR: (Throwing up hands) Oh, great!

RICK: I mean, I knew it was coming. But now that it's really here—

DOCTOR: (Interrupting with an air of resignation) You're done.

RICK: I mean *really* here, we're going to have to— (pause)—hm?

DOCTOR: You're done.

RICK: Done?

DOCTOR: Done.

RICK: Oh, come on. It's not *that* bad.

DOCTOR: (Ironic) Oh, no. Not at all. That is, if you like being unemployed.

RICK: (Getting more upset) Unemployed? No. That won't happen. Carter said I wouldn't be laid off.

DOCTOR: And you believe him, I suppose.

RICK: Of course, I belie—of *course* I believe him. Shouldn't I?

DOCTOR: Rick, you're gonna lose your job.

RICK: My job?

DOCTOR: Yeah. Your job, your house, your marriage . . . your dog.

RICK: My dog!?

DOCTOR: All of it. Gone.

RICK: What do I do?

DOCTOR: Not much. (Beat) But, there are a few things you might wanna try, I guess—for whatever good it'll do.

RICK: What?

DOCTOR: Well, to start, you've gotta stop meeting with Carter.

RICK: Stop meeting with him? Why?

DOCTOR: Why? Did you *enjoy* that last little meeting?

RICK: No.

DOCTOR: So, stop punishing yourself.

RICK: But I have to talk to him. He's my boss.

DOCTOR: Okay, fine. But when you do, let him do the talking. If he asks how things are going, say, "Fine."

RICK: Fine.

DOCTOR: And if he asks if you have got any problems, say, "No problems."

RICK: No problems.

DOCTOR: There. Now you've got it. It'll save a lot of wear and tear on your ego.

RICK: (Practicing) Fine. No problems.

DOCTOR: Play it cool. Keep your head down. And then, when he gets ready to fire some managers, he won't even remember who you are.

RICK: Okay, but what about my people? That meeting I had the other day was a disaster, and my individual talks with them—well, they were a little better, but I'm still not sure how they're doing.

DOCTOR: Rick. Hey, dealing with your people. That's the easy part.

RICK: It is?

DOCTOR: Of course. Just take their side.

RICK: Their side?

DOCTOR: Of course. Tell them that upper management *made* you do it. They'll feel sorry for you.

RICK: You're saying I don't have to be committed to it?

DOCTOR: Noooo. They'll respect you more if you aren't. You'll be one of them—at least until this thing blows over.

RICK: You're sure this will work?

DOCTOR: Rick. Trust me. And don't forget your nickel.

RICK: Oh, yeah.

In this segment, you see Rick at the low point in the change process. First there was his unsuccessful meeting with his people—the one you saw in Chapter 2. Then there were his one-on-one meetings with his people, which went pretty well. Then, after the last meeting with Carter, Rick bottomed out. He became transparent.

His progression to this state, like that of Paul, Judy, and Warren, is by degrees. He actually starts out taking some ownership of the situation, but in his emotionally weakened condition, he succumbs quickly to the "Doctor's" pushing all his buttons.

First, there was Carter. He was a convenient target. Rick convinced himself quickly that he might as well give up trying to deal with management. After all, hadn't he tried? Hadn't he done his level best to be responsive and responsible to the overall corporate decisions and goals?

True, he has reason to be frustrated. He appears, in fact, to have shown more responsibility to the organization and Carter than they have to him. But the decision to "cut his losses" and look out for himself is *his* choice, a decision he arrives at with himself. Those decisions make good martyrs, but bad managers.

In dealing with his employees, he also talks himself into a course of action that is not in his or their best interests. Granted, he can get sympathy, but that is only a short-term gain. The long-term results of siding with employees against upper management is that ultimately the manager is seen as *one* of the employees and is, therefore, cut off from management in general. As a result, the manager, on whom the employees pinned their hopes, is now dead weight. The lifeline that the manager represented has now been cut.

In this scenario, no one denies that Rick or any manager in that position does not have good cause to withdraw and become invisible. But good cause is not the same as an excuse. Therefore, it takes a rather substantial effort of the will for many managers in a changing environment to withstand the temptation to fade into invisibility.

Moreover, as you saw in Rick's case, the effects of that kind of disengagement reach far beyond the job. Regardless of how much Rick tries to convince himself that he is justified, a part of him knows better—knows the truth and knows, if only generally, the long-term effects of self-deception.

Already he is beginning to play out that scenario. His job, his house, his marriage—he realizes they are all potentially on the line. Although treated somewhat humorously in this scenario, these effects are quite real. When there is disruptive change in organizations, there is a corresponding drop in the domestic well-being of its employees.

In a change situation, the first-line managers and supervisors are probably the most vulnerable of any of the organization's employees. They are vulnerable because they are targets. They are the organization's version of the battlefield's first lieutenants whose average life expectancy, after the first sighting of the enemy, is measured in seconds. The ultimate irony for the managers is that much of what they experience is what they, in effect, "choose" because of the self-defeating conversations they have with themselves.

THE SELF-MANAGEMENT PROCESS

Now that Rick, Warren, Judy, and Paul have dug themselves into a hole, the question becomes, "How do they get out?" The answer to this question is basically the same answer given for how they got there in the first place—self-talk.

In the following scenario, you will see Warren, fresh from his meeting with Rick, feeling good about the blows he struck for truth and justice. This time, however, the response will be different. The convention has been changed so that this time, instead of getting bad advice, Warren will get some good advice.

What follows is a dramatization of *positive* or *constructive self-talk*. As such, it provides the model for a self-management technique—an interpersonal tool you can use to break the momentum of negative thinking and begin to move toward accepting change. As you read the dialogue, you will hear Warren ask himself a number of questions. Mentally note which ones strike you as key to this process.

Picture the following: Warren returns to the psychiatrist's stand jauntily, the picture of self-confidence. The "Doctor" is dressed a little differently than before; he is more "together."

DOCTOR: Well, how did it go?

WARREN: Great! Boy, did I tell *him*. Ha. He hardly got a word in edgewise.

DOCTOR: Really gave it to him, huh?

WARREN: And how! He deserved it!

DOCTOR: You sound angry.

WARREN: I *am* angry.

DOCTOR: How's it working for you?

WARREN: (Double take) Hm?

DOCTOR: (Getting angry) How's it working for you?

WARREN: How's it working—(interrupts himself, stands up, hands on counter, looks around behind and under the stand as if looking for some-body else) Hey, wait. You're not the same one I—Where'd he go?

DOCTOR: (More forcefully) How's it working, Warren?

WARREN: (Defensive; bravado) Like I said, great. They needed to be told, so I told them. Simple.

DOCTOR: Um hm. (Pause, more conciliatory) Look, Warren. Let me ask you something.

WARREN: (Less defensive, but still a little wary) Sure, go ahead.

DOCTOR: I realize this change is pretty disruptive—to everybody. And they don't like it. But in your case—aside from just getting mad—what are you telling yourself—specifically? What are you concerned about losing?

WARREN: (Energized) Losing! Are you kidding?! I'm losing everything!

DOCTOR: Like?

WARREN: (Starts to tick them off on his fingers) Effi-ciency. I mean this new system is crazy. And communication—between me and the peo-ple I work with—not to mention the drop in productivity we're experiencing (pauses; leans closer)—and, well, frankly, if you ask me, that's going to sink us—not to mention our whole department. It's like when my co-workers come to me, I can't help 'em. We're working in a vacuum. They've cut us off at the knees.

DOCTOR: Sounds pretty grim.

WARREN: You said it!

DOCTOR: Now tell me. Is all that true?

WARREN: Is what true?

DOCTOR: All of the things you mentioned. That the new system will sink you, that you're helpless to help the people you work with, that "they've" cut you off at the knees.

WARREN: Well, I suppose not totally—(quickly)—but our productivity *is* down and confusion is definitely up.

DOCTOR: True. Those things are happening. But to repeat, is the company going under—and are you all totally helpless, like you said?

WARREN: Well, no, not really.

DOCTOR: Okay, then. Let me ask this. What do you want? What would you like to gain from all this?

WARREN: Gain?

DOCTOR: Yes.

WARREN: (Slowly, then more quickly) Well, I don't know—I suppose one thing we might be able to gain is a more efficient system for doing some things that used to be a real headache—(interrupts himself)—yeah, as a matter of fact, we could do a lot of things differently.— In terms of the information I need, well, I guess I'm just going to have to bite the bullet and get up to speed on those new areas as fast as I can.

DOCTOR: What's the first step you could take?

WARREN: The first step. Well, maybe the best thing to do is talk to Rollie. He's more familiar with this whole thing than I am, and he knows basically what our operation is like—so yeah, I think talking to him would be the logical first step.

DOCTOR: Sounds great. Do it.

WARREN: Thanks. I will. Oh, by the way, you want a nickel?

DOCTOR: Naw. This advice is on the house.

In this scenario, Warren was able to turn himself around. Granted it may have seemed a little too easy, but this is only a dramatization. The actual process he modeled tends to cover more ground, but the method is valid.

In response to the question, "Which of the 'Doctor's' questions seemed to be key to this interaction?" two questions get the most votes:

- Is it true?
- What is the first step you could take?

The question, "Is it true?" is the retort to the earlier questions, "What are you telling yourself? What do you fear losing?" This retort is the acid test. It tends to break the momentum of negative self-talk.

The question, "What's the first step you could take?" is likewise the follow-up to the question, "What do you want to gain?" It forces the person to shift gears and translate ideas into actions. The process as a whole is described next.

Ask yourself the following questions:

1. What am I telling myself about the change? (What do I fear losing?)
2. Is it really true?

Then you have to examine your real wants and needs. Ask yourself:

3. What do I really want from this change? (What would I like to gain?)

Finally, you need to take action. Determine:

4. What first step can I take to gain what I want?

Now consider the logic of the process:

1. *What am I telling myself about the change? What do I fear losing?*

This is usually the easiest of the questions to answer. Most people can answer it quickly. People are very good at identifying what they do not like about a change situation.

This process is similar to the grieving process in which people, before they can begin to overcome a loss, must first get in touch emotionally with the reality of the loss. Far from being an exercise in focusing on the negative, it is an essential step in clarifying the ending.

The next logical question might seem to be, "What would I like to gain?" But another question needs to be asked first:

2. *Is it really true? Is everything you've been saying about what you've lost really true?*

This is a key question because it is the reality test. More often than not the answer is "No." People tend to exaggerate. As you saw in the self-talk scenes, people allow negative statements to chain together and push the limits of credulity. Often this process is more an expression of an emotional response than a factual reality. But you need to remind yourself of this fact. When asked, "Is it really true?" people are likely to say, "Well, no."

For example, someone might say, "I'm going to lose my job," when in reality the likelihood is very remote. On the other hand, it might really be true. If it is, it is good to know that. You may tell yourself two things, both of which are catastrophic. On examination, you find out that one is not true, you exaggerated it. But the other one *is* true. That is something you really *do* need to worry about. It is important to know which one is true and which one is not.

Is it true? is a key question, because it can break the momentum of any negative self-talk you have going and put it in the light of reality. Only by breaking or cracking that mold can you answer the next question. If you jump from question 1 to question 3, you may be trying to answer the question with inaccurate or false information.

3. *What do I really want from this change? What would I like to gain?*

When people begin to see that they can gain, they begin turning the corner. The "gain" question allows people to focus on the potential advantage of the change. Initially the answers to this question may be general, vague, or superficial. But the more you press it, the more specific and realistic the answers become. This question helps the mind remember what it has known all along, but may have shelved in favor of the more energy-laden loss statements. Asking this question is a way of retraining or rebalancing your mind.

4.   *What first step can I take to gain what I want?*

There is a kind of euphoria here, a real happiness in the sense that you are looking at the positive side of things now. It takes an equal shift of mental gears to answer this one, "What could you do to get that going?" In a change situation, first steps are more important from a psychological and motivational point of view than from an accomplishment point of view. Finally, you feel like you are moving forward. Even though in the grand scheme of things a single step is not very much, at the beginning of the change process, a single step is a great deal. It is a symbol of your changed point of view and your commitment to move on.

PUTTING THE SELF-MANAGEMENT PROCESS TO WORK

The term self-management process would indicate that it is a skill that you could practice on your own—and it is. It can also be practiced in partnership with someone else. In either case, it has proven to be a simple and effective method to enable you to (1) cut through any false information you may be telling yourself and (2) establish a foothold in the process of moving to beginnings.

The process of practicing the skill alone is best understood in light of the process done in partnership with someone else. At Wilson Learning, we have had a great deal of experience and success using the Partner Interview. In this exercise, two people "interview" each other using the four questions of the process. Person 1, for example, asks Person 2, "What are you telling yourself about change? Specifically, what do you fear losing?"

Person 2 answers the question. Then Person 1 proceeds to ask and receive answers to the next three questions. At that point, the two people switch and Person 2 interviews Person 1.

The results of this exercise are often surprising to both people. They tend to go into the exercise feeling that they will not learn any more than they already know. They come out of it with a very different point of view. Common responses include:

- "I thought I knew how I felt about this matter, but having to explain it to someone else brought out facets I guess I had felt, but had never really clarified."
- "I learned things about myself I didn't know before."
- "I felt pretty much that my basic problem with the change was just getting up to speed on the new systems marketing procedure, but I found in talking about it that my real concern was a fear, I guess you'd call it, of not being able to keep up with new procedures in general—of being passed up by younger people who are more comfortable with these systems than I am."
- "I thought I was disoriented. I discovered I am disidentified."

Another set of common responses focus on the role of catalyst played by the partner:

- "She came up with ideas I never would have thought of."
- "I can lie to myself, but I couldn't lie to him."
- "Just the pressure of having to explain it—that made me think the whole thing through more than I normally would."

The two primary themes of participant comments are:

1. *Specificity.* The process forces people to specify what otherwise would remain vague and, therefore, not something which the person could easily take action to correct or implement.

2. *Emotional versus Technical.* People often begin to describe some technical or procedural problem or issue and

end up discovering that the issue they began with was only a symptom for the deeper emotional core issue.

The success of the self-management process when done in controlled pairs raises the question, "Can the same process be done alone in a noncontrolled situation?" The answer is, "Yes," but it is more difficult. To use the technique effectively on your own requires discipline and practice. When people fail to be able to make it work for them, it is usually more the result of lack of discipline than the fault of the process.

The questions themselves are carefully designed to quickly and specifically identify endings and move the participant into the transition/beginnings process.

After his meeting with Carter and his self-defeating talk with himself, Rick decided to talk to his colleague, John. The conversation will not be dramatized here, but the basic conclusions Rick reached are as follows:

1. *What am I telling myself about the change? What do I fear losing?*

   A. The change is terrible.
   B. I feel that upper management doesn't trust us.
   C. I am going to lose my job.
   D. I am going to lose my position.
   E. I am going to lose the respect of my people.
   F. They are going to find out how incompetent I really am.
   G. I am going to get totally lost.
   H. I cannot handle a change of this scope.

2. *Is it really true?*

   A. Sort of.
   B. Probably not.
   C. No.
   D. Maybe.
   E. Maybe.
   F. No.
   G. Probably not.
   H. Not true.

In general, Rick discovered three basic things:

- My worry about losing my job, being incompetent, and unable to handle the change are unfounded exaggerations.
- I could lose my position if I don't perform up to the company's expectations. This loss of position would come in the form of a lateral move to a position with less likelihood for future promotions.
- Acceptance by my people is very important to my self-esteem, not to mention its effect on the productivity of our department.

3. *What do I really want from this change? What do I want to gain?*

- I would like to use this change as an opportunity to bring the department members more closely together as a team so that we can be productive and unified, and can have fun.
- I want to be recognized by my boss and my colleagues as a creative and highly effective manager.
- I want our department to work out a functioning system within six months.

4. *What's the first step I can take to gain what I want?*

Rick identified three first steps:

- Meet with all my people one-on-one and find out what their specific needs are.
- Outline a short-term strategy to present to Carter for discussion and feedback. Don't make demands on him; ask his opinion.
- Set a day aside to meet with John and develop a concurrent strategy for combining Levels One and Four.

Rick expressed his overall reaction to his own self-management process as follows:

> The main thing that surprised me was how important acceptance is to me. It sounds sort of egotistical, but after talking about it, I had to admit that recognition, a sense of unity in

the department, and Carter's respect were a lot more important than I thought. That's what I *really* want out of work.

The fact that I decided to develop two strategies—one brief,
for Carter, and a more detailed one with John—didn't surprise
me. Those were logical steps. But what struck me is that in
simply writing down that I was going to do those things, by or
on specific dates, gave me a peace of mind that seemed to be
out of proportion to the simplicity of the suggestion.

Finally, I am very concerned about these one-on-one meetings with my people. I want them to go well.

As Rick's example serves to illustrate, the deceptively simple self-management process can have very substantial and
positive effects.

FEAR VERSUS ANXIETY

You may remember from a psychology class or from reading
that the technical difference between fear and anxiety is that
fear has an object; anxiety does not. If you are afraid to leave
your house because you think you will be mugged—that is
fear. But if you are just plain afraid to leave your house—that
is anxiety.

Given a choice of having fear or anxiety, the obvious choice
is fear. With fear, at least you know what to look out for. When
you know what it is you are afraid of, when you have an
object, then you also can begin to think about how to deal
with it. You can start by looking for solutions. In contrast, if
you are anxious, you cannot focus your action or look for
solutions because you do not know what you are dealing with.

This distinction is well illustrated by the basic structure of
fairy tales dealing with the phenomenon of "calling out the
dragon." These tales generally begin with a sense that there is
something terribly wrong in the land: The crops are not growing, the livestock are barren, and there is drought and disease.
Usually, the reason for this state of affairs is unknown, but
its concrete manifestation is rumored to be a monster, some
kind of dragon living in the mountains or the woods. Then in
a vision, a person—often a young man—is chosen to confront
the unknown creature. When the young man, dressed as a

knight, finally discovers the monster's lair, he ritualistically "calls out the dragon"—he demands that it appear—and the dragon, following the convention of the fairy-tale tradition, presents itself. The young man's initial reaction is usually shock, "WOW! That's a *big* dragon!"

At this point, anxiety (not knowing what the monster was) is transformed into fear. But out in the open, the young man knows what he is up against. His anxious foreboding turns to resolve, and even though the dragon is formidable, the young man usually has a secret trick or strategy to defeat it.

This prototype of the classic fairy tale is a succinct expression of an experience of change. As long as the change remains an unknown, rumor-laden, nonspecific threat, the organization will be like the kingdom in the fairy tale—unproductive. But as more and more people "call out the dragon"—that is, specify the problem—they will be able to define objects and then, as if by magic, come up with creative and innovative ways of dealing with those problems.

Good self-management, like good counseling in general, has the same purpose, first to transform anxiety into fear, that is, to bring the actual problem into focus so you can deal with it. When you are honest with yourself, you tend to discover that the concerns you have are not as horrible as your self-talk has led you to believe. What may at first appear to be numerous dragons generally turns out to be a manageable number.

Once you have yourself "managed," you are in a much stronger position to help your co-workers deal with change, the focus of the next chapter.

7

TRANSITIONS: THE CSE SUPPORT SYSTEM

It [the neutral zone] is, as they say,
a great place to visit, but you
wouldn't want to live there.
William Bridges

The modern world view of transition is that it is "a kind of street-crossing procedure. One would be a fool to stay out there in the middle of the street any longer than was necessary, so once you step off the curb, move on to the other side as fast as you can. And whatever you do, don't sit down on the center line to think things over!" (Bridges, pp. 112–113). But, as previously noted, for a successful ending and, consequently, a successful new beginning, people need to take time for transitions. The question is, "How much time?" The answer, "Until you begin to see movement, and then only as often as is necessary to keep the movement going." Remember, the process of dealing with endings is to a certain extent static. You want to get a fix on where *you* are and where others are regarding the change. The key endings question, "How does change affect me and my co workers?" assumes a stationary target. The key question for transitions is different:

How do I move myself and other people toward beginnings?

An operative word in this question is *move*. That movement may be slow or fast, but the goal is some kind of movement. You cannot be responsible for solving everyone's problems. Moreover, in a change situation, you usually will not be solving problems, but removing barriers, providing support, and establishing direction for both yourself and others.

In the Never End exercise you discovered that people in change have three basic needs. The first is *empathy* —someone to listen and share your feelings. The second is *understanding* an intellectual grasp of what happened and what is going to happen. And third is *ideas*, specific suggestions for moving on. These are the basic needs—what people find useful—when going through change.

The skill that follows is a strategy designed to help you provide these solutions. The model itself is a simple counseling procedure that can be tailored to the individual needs of the people you work with. It will enable you to help them to become aware of, and then to generate, a plan for moving toward accepting change. This strategy is called the CSE (Clarify, Share, Engage) Support System.

Think again about the key question associated with transitions, "How do I move myself and other people toward beginnings?" More than just movement, it also has a great deal to do with reorienting. The skills encompassed in the CSE Support System will not solve all your problems once and for all. They are *not* a panacea. But they can help you start the process of beginning to accept and participate in change. The CSE Support System can help you to create an environment that supports individuals who are moving through a change. It helps you provide the basic needs individuals have identified as important to their pathway through change.

CLARIFY

The first step in the CSE Support System is to clarify specific issues and concerns. During this step you can test your hypothesis of the problem(s) individuals may be having with change. This involves three integrated activities: listening, focusing, and restating.

Listening

Listening is an important part of the process to help you and your co-workers end an attachment with the past. Indeed, listening is probably the single most important skill in the change process. But what *is* listening? Closing your mouth and opening your ears? Yes, but it is also a great deal more.

Most of us are taught that listening is a passive skill. Good communication, however, takes energy. It takes energy to focus on what the other person is saying or *not saying*.

Communication, specifically listening, is also a behavior. It can be taught, learned, changed, or improved. Research indicates, however, that in instances when one individual or group tries to change another individual or group, the side advocating the change usually talks 80 percent of the time and listens to the opposing side only 20 percent of the time. It is far more effective, however, to *listen* to the reasons for the opposition, providing a basis on which to build more viable arguments.

In change situations where people are having difficulty ending an attachment to the past, you need to listen actively both for what is said and what is *not* said (verbal and nonverbal communication). If people are demonstrating resistance to change, you have to listen carefully to their concerns if you are going to support them and help them accept and commit to the change.

Listening is hard work. People do not take to it naturally. To demonstrate this to yourself, find someone and ask them to talk for a minute about something that has happened recently, something that has both facts and feelings. Pick something out of everyday experience: a frustrating encounter with a rude waiter, a funny experience with a child, a rewarding experience with someone you love. Keep it real; keep it simple. Once the experience has been selected, let that person talk for a few minutes while you listen and then summarize back to that person—to his or her satisfaction—what was said. Then switch roles, with you talking and the other person listening.

The results of this exercise are always enlightening. When you are the listener (summarizer) you will probably find the following:

- It was hard work.
- There was tension because you felt obligated to get all the facts and feelings.
- Your mind was at full attention—in overdrive.
- You realize that you do not normally listen at that level.

This last insight is the most important. Ordinarily people are passive listeners. They hear, but they do not necessarily remember or assimilate the information. But in the exercise just described, you became an active listener—putting your energy into it simply because when the person is through speaking, *you are accountable*. You have to repeat it back to that person's satisfaction.

On the other hand, when you were the receiver, when the other person summarized to you, how did that feel? It probably felt good knowing somebody went to the effort to really try to understand you to the point of being able to summarize your message back. Now consider, how often does that happen to you? Probably not very often. The process is a cut above what normally passes for listening.

Now consider the process of summarizing and how that can be made most effective. For example, someone says, "Well, last week our daughter went to college. It was a lot of fun because she was excited about going, and then the next day we noticed the house was quiet and we started to miss her. It was kind of a unique experience for my wife and me."

Here's what the feedback might be. "If I get what you're talking about, last week your daughter went to college, and you were all feeling happy and there was a lot of excitement before she went, good feelings, and you didn't realize there'd be a letdown the next day. When you woke up and she wasn't there, you felt very nostalgic. Either that or maybe sadness?" The main difference between the statement and the restatement is that in the statement the feelings were by-and-large implied, but not stated explicitly. In the feedback, however, the feelings were stated explicitly in the form of questions. Was it sadness? Nostalgia?

If you're giving feedback to people you work with, for example, you are saying in effect, "What I thought I heard was that you were mad about that. Is that true? Or is it just sad? Or is it frustration? What is the name of the emotion you are having?" When people actually commit to a feeling word, although the feelings are very present, the intellectual commitment to a word helps them understand it, too. "Yes, I hadn't thought about it in those terms, but now that you mention it, I guess I was more frustrated than mad." It's important to recognize the difference between *implied* and *stated* feelings.

In general, listening as defined here is another example of a general theme promoted throughout this book, namely the value of making the unknown known; of making the vague explicit; of not taking things for granted or making assumptions without checking them out. Much of the problem of change stems from a fear of the unknown in the form of rumors, exaggerations, assumptions, and ill-defined feelings. By naming the feelings, putting a mirror up to the rumors, and challenging the assumptions and exaggerations, however, you bring the issues to light. You may not like what you see, but at least you know what it is.

Focusing

While you are listening, your job is to help the individual focus on his or her position in the change process. In this step you ask questions to help pinpoint the real issues. Focusing is not only honing down, it is also selecting. When people talk, they will probably cover a lot of issues. Your job is to select the key issues at the heart of their responses to the change. The simplest and most effective way to do this is through the same questions you used in the self-management process, "What do you fear losing? What do you want to gain?" They may include a number of issues that do not have anything to do with the change. At this point you focus on only the things that are part of the change.

Assume a manager in a change environment has an employee named Jim. After carefully listening to him, the manager identifies four basic concerns: loss of his (1) job, (2) competence, (3) budget, and (4) team members.

Notice that the first of these fears doesn't mesh with the rest. If he loses his job, he will not have to worry about his competence, his budget, or his team members. When faced with a summary of his fears, Jim may quickly dismiss the first one, saying, "Well, I guess losing my job is fairly unlikely, but the other fears are not." Already the "mirror method" is exposing some of the fears as unfounded. But the others are real and need to be addressed. Before addressing them, however, it is useful to ask the second question. "What would you like to gain?"

As stated earlier, people will give one of three basic responses. One answers immediately, "Well, I could gain this,

this, and this." They list off things with ease. A second type of person, who is shifting of gears, answers, "Well, let's see, I don't know, I suppose I could gain this and this and this." In other words, they have to think about it a little bit. It is an effort, but they do see gains. The third type of response is, "Gain? Are you kidding? There's nothing to gain!"

How people answer the question about gain is one of the best indicators in terms of where they are on the change scale and how easy or difficult it may be to get them moving.

Once you are able to focus on a sense of loss and a hoped-for gain, you will be able to begin removing the barriers to moving toward that change. This ability is especially important in the second phase of the change process—the transition—as individuals are detaching from the past and trying to identify their real wants and interests.

By far the most difficult part of the listening/focusing process is to keep your own ideas out of it. You are trying to help them define, for themselves, what *they* see as the problem, concern, or opportunity. Even though you may be chomping at the bit to tell them, enlighten them, disagree with them, or set them straight—don't. Empathize and let them work out the understanding. If you try to shortcut that method, you will be guilty of jumping to beginnings. The listening process is the finale of the ending and the entrance into the transition.

Restating

Usually toward the end of the clarify process, you can use the communication technique of restating, previously described in the discussion of summarizing. Restating helps people share information that may be difficult for them. By restating what you understood, you give others a chance to hear what they have said. In fact, often people are not sure what they are trying to say. Hearing it restated by someone else can help them clarify their real interests.

The "acid test" of listening is restating or summarizing, to the speaker's satisfaction, what the speaker has just said. This will establish the empathy people need as they are moving through change.

In all, the clarification step of the support system helps people identify what they fear losing and enables them to determine their real interests in the change issue.

SHARE

The second step of the CSE Support System is sharing. Sharing is simply giving the person you are talking to your understanding of what is happening. Remember that the second thing people want as they are moving through change is intellectual understanding. Once you have helped clarify what people fear losing (most likely it is some attachment to form or the past) and what they might gain, you are ready to help them see what is going on, what has happened to them.

In this step you are shifting gears. Whereas the speaker was the focus in the clarify step, now it is your turn. In the sharing step, you help the person understand how his or her interests fit with the company's purpose. In essence, you make the match.

Communicating the purpose of the change in relation to that person's stated interests can persuade the person to look at the situation differently. For someone experiencing change, sharing is very important. Through it you pave the way for them to focus on the purpose and discover what they can gain from the change.

The sharing phase has five specific steps:

1. *Signal the shift.* Remember, in the clarify state, the person has been talking, and you have been listening. They have been doing almost 90 percent of the talking, and you have been going along with them. Now suddenly you turn it around, and you are going to be doing the talking. Unless you tell them that is what you are doing and why, it could come off as, "Well, thank you for baring your soul, David. I'm very touched. But now I'd like to tell you what we're *really* here for." Although exaggerated, that kind of statement is one possible conclusion people might draw. But if you simply say something like, "Okay, now that I have an understanding of what you're feeling, what I'd

like to do, if you don't mind, is take the spotlight for a while and explain some of the things that are going on that are related to the concerns you've just expressed." A statement like that tells them there is going to be a shift. If you do not do that, they might draw the wrong conclusion.

2. *Explain the purpose of your information.*   State that you want to explain the why and how of the change and how it relates specifically to the needs they expressed. It is essential that what you share be linked to what the person said; otherwise it will seem that your listening was just a perfunctory gesture.

3. *Overview the change in general.*   A short history of the change will suffice, just an outline. Remember, your purpose here is to address their concerns, not hold forth at length on your opinions and theories. Although oversimplified here, the share process is essentially an integrating process. On the one hand are the person's stated fears and hoped-for gains; on the other hand, the facts—as far as you know them—of the change. The process: Use the facts to address the fears and hopes. Whether it is good news, bad news, or no news, the person will appreciate the effort and honesty you make to systematically address the issues.

4. *Then link it to their concerns.*   Make a connection between what the individual wants to gain and the new direction of the change. "You just told me that you have four basic concerns, and I just outlined the general change. Let's see how it stacks up against the four concerns you have." If you do not do this step, you can get a very negative reaction. If you explain the change and how the company is doing but you do not relate it to their concerns, they will wonder why they told you in the first place.

5. *Net it out.*   Jim's manager might say, "Jim, you have basically four concerns: Number one is losing your job. Don't worry about that. Management has assured me that your job is secure. Number two, being incompetent on the new job will be addressed through training. You will probably have to struggle for a while, but you'll get it. And you will

be in the same boat as everybody else. In terms of number three, getting the budget you want, that's a toss-up. We don't know right now. I think I can get you most of what you have asked for, but I'm not sure at this point. And number four, in terms of keeping the team together, I'm sorry, but that just isn't in the cards."

Avoid the tendency to evaluate or judge. If you suggest a "better" idea or "the" answer, you will not only kill the process, but very likely eliminate some very good ideas you have not thought of.

ENGAGE

The third need of people during a change is direction—suggestions on steps to take. Therefore, the final phase of the CSE Support System is to engage. This third step is where you gain the individual's commitment to take ownership of the change and attach to the new beginnings. In this step you develop future-focused action steps that enable the person to move toward the change. If you help someone all the way through the change process but do not gain a commitment for action, then you have not reached your objective.

To engage people in the change process, you need to have first followed the CSE Support System. If you have effectively clarified and shared, they will be ready to take ownership of the change.

The engage phase of the CSE process has four specific steps.

1. *Ask for understanding and agreement.* "Is everything we've talked about so far clear?" This question will basically tie a bow on the share stage. "Before we move on to actually dealing with this, do you understand the change and how it lines up with your concerns? Have I left anything out here?" Make sure the person is with you before you move on.

2. *Ask them for ideas.* "Given that, do you have any ideas of things we could do?" Get their ideas out. Discuss them. Honor them. Do not evaluate or judge them.

3. *Suggest ideas.*   "Okay, here's some ideas I have." In many cases it may be the same as the ones they have. Or you may have a few new ideas.

4. *Agree to finite steps.*   Agree on which ideas are the best, and then agree to an action plan and set another meeting date to check progress. "Okay then, we agree that you're going to project out staffing needs in terms of budget, determine what has to be done and see if you can divide that up among the people you've got. You have three people who've got to start doing the work of six. See if you can somehow get a sense of who is going to do what. Let's get back in a week. I'd like to see your ideas about the people and the budget. In the meantime, I'll try to find out what the actual number on that budget is, and I'll also set up the training for you."

Gaining commitment to *act* is essential at this point. You will also want to set up some kind of ongoing feedback or monitoring system.

**A word of caution: Do not be overly
ambitious in the action plan.**

When people are hit with a change, they are often caught off guard, so you do not want to try to map out a huge master plan. There are two reasons why you do not want to do that. One, they have enough to handle. It is better just to work with getting the next steps identified. What about tomorrow? Plus the fact that any master plan in the changing environment probably is going to change itself, so the effort would be wasted. Both the psychological and practical reasons prevent that action.

This process is analogous to going across a creek on stepping stones. Your purpose is to get to the other side, but you must focus on the stones, one stone at a time. You test the first stone to make sure it is solid before you put your weight on it. Then when you are standing solidly on that one, you focus on the next one. Now, have you forgotten in the meantime that your purpose is to get to the other side? No. But your focus is down there on those stones. It may take you in a route different than the one you thought you were going to take to get across. Instead of a straight line across, it may take you up and down the stream a little bit. But you have to go where the stones are solid.

IN SUMMARY

The CSE Support System can be summarized as follows:

> C = Clarify Perceived Loss/Real Wants
> S = Share Gain/Purpose of the Change
> E = Engage Commitment to the Change

The contours of this process are:

Clarify

1. *Listen.*   Actively listen to the employee's questions, concerns, gripes, opinions, and feelings. Based on what you have heard, clarify the employee's sense of loss and hoped-for gain.
2. *Focus.*   Hone in on the issues that apply to the change situation.
3. *Restate.*   Summarize the information you have received to the speaker's satisfaction.

Clarifying meets people's need for empathy.

Share

1. *Signal the shift.*   Let the other person know you will be shifting from listening to talking.
2. *Explain the purpose.* Explain the change and then match it to their concerns and needs.
3. *Overview the change.*   Explain your understanding of the new system and the employee's new position or opportunities in that system. Be brief.

4. *Link to their concerns.*   Use the general information to address each of their concerns.
5. *Net it out.*   Spell out specifically how their concerns will be met or not met, and if you do not know whether they will be met, say so.

Sharing meets people's need for intellectual understanding.

Engage

1. *Ask for understanding/agreement.*   Make sure you both agree on the information exchanged thus far.
2. *Ask them for ideas.*   Solicit ideas from the other person. Do not judge or evaluate.
3. *Suggest ideas.*   Contribute your own ideas.
4. *Agree to finite steps.*   Select which ideas you both agree on and establish action steps.

Engaging meets people's need for first steps to take.

In summary, the CSE Support System has two main stages. The first is the clarify stage. In this stage the responsibility is to focus on the concerns of others. The second stage is the share/engage stage. This stage is, in effect, "your turn," your opportunity to explain the new system or plan and engage the people with whom you work in taking an active and supportive role in it.

The success of this second stage is clearly dependent on the first. If you have not listened well and established a sense of trust, your "sharing" will appear self-serving and your "engaging" will appear manipulative.

CONCLUSION

The CSE Support System is a common-sense intervention strategy that you can use primarily for helping other people through the change process. Its simplicity is its greatest strength and its greatest weakness. Because it is simple, it can be implemented quickly and effectively. That is its strength. But its simplicity can also be a weakness. If, for example, you see it as an add-water-and-stir solution to problems, you will be disappointed. Understanding it is one thing; making it work is another. Also, it can be adapted to a manager-employer or a peer-peer interaction.

THE CSE SUPPORT SYSTEM AT AVERCO

The CSE Support System provides a "generic counseling" approach to helping people manage change. Two of Rick's people at Averco, Dennis and Peggy, are moving toward the change rather easily, or so it appears, but they still need support and encouragement. Too often management focuses attention on those employees who are experiencing great difficulties and ignores the comparatively minor problems of those making the adjustment more easily.

To see the "generic version" of the CSE Support System, listen in on a conversation between Rick and Dennis.

RICK: I know you've been floating around a lot, but I wanted to get back to you to be sure everything was okay.

DENNIS: I appreciate it. Things are going well. It's a lot of work, but John's been really helpful answering questions. Things are moving along as smooth as I could hope for.

RICK: Is there anything? Any specific questions that I might be able to help with from my end?

DENNIS: Well, one thing, recently I've been spending a lot of my time with marketing—much more so than creative. And I was just curious. Was that the intention of my move, I mean, was that what you hoped I'd get into?

RICK: You're covering a lot more in the marketing area?

DENNIS: Yes.

RICK: I think that pans out just about the way we thought it was going to work out. So that's what they want. I'm glad to hear that.

DENNIS: Yes, it's exciting. Like I said, I feel real green about it, but it's starting to come.

RICK: Good, You want to be sure you help the other
          folks. I'm seeing people's eyes clearing and
          brightening as the days go by.

DENNIS: I was also concerned about the order of priori-
          ties. I don't want them to feel like I'm shorting
          them with the time spent with them.

RICK: Not at all. In fact, I've heard comments from
          most of those folks that they appreciate the
          bits and pieces you're feeding them.

DENNIS: Great.

RICK: They really appreciate the way you've helped
          them. In fact, you've helped us define some
          areas we really didn't anticipate being prob-
          lems. Thanks!

DENNIS: Thank *you.*

Notice that Rick checked with Dennis to see how he was
doing. He drew him out, listened to what he was saying, and
asked if he had any questions. He then clarified, "So you're
spending more time in marketing?" He confirmed that what
Dennis was doing was in line with Rick's understanding,
"That pans out just about the way we thought it was going to
work out." He reinforced him, "I've heard comments from
most of those folks that they appreciate the bits and pieces
you're feeding them." And he thanked Dennis for his good
work.

Statistically, if you had a choice of working with the people
who have problems and those who do not, if you had to work
with one or the other, you would be better off working with
the ones who do not have problems. Very often, however, the
squeaky wheel gets the grease. In a change situation, people
who are moving toward the new beginnings need CSE just as
often, maybe not as much, but just as often as those who are
having problems.

Next listen in on a conversation between Rick and Peggy,
the other member of his team who is having no problem herself, but whose behavior is not very accepted by the other
members of the team. Watch for the elements of the CSE Support System in this conversation.

RICK: So, Peg, basically what I'm hearing you say is that things are going smoothly, all things considered, and that you feel pretty good about it, right?

PEG: Yeah. I feel great about the changes that are going on. But like I said before, I feel like the odd person. I've noticed everybody else has this sort of negativity and, I don't know, it's just frustrating that they're not grabbing the chances that are waiting for them.

RICK: Is there some tension between you and the rest of the group?

PEG: Yes, there is.

RICK: Let me ask you this. If there was something that you were working on that you really didn't like and the rest of the group that was working with you was behind it 100 percent, totally, how would that make you feel?

PEG: I wouldn't like that very much. Is that what I've been doing?

RICK: Maybe just a little bit.

PEG: Yeah, but I'm like that, you know.

RICK: I know, and the energy and the enthusiasm you bring to things is one of the things that's so great about you. But how about using that in a different direction? How about taking that energy and maybe using it to help some of the others get behind it and maybe even understand it better?

PEG: Yes. I can see that. You know, I really understand what we're trying to go for, and perhaps if I sat down with people and really went specifically over it, that might help them understand it further. You know, I might sit down and talk with Warren. I mean really talk with him instead of talking *at* him. Instead of being a cheerleader about the thing. Really try to be with people.

RICK: Sounds good to me. Listen, let me tell you again. I really appreciate your attitude and the job you're doing.

PEG: Thanks. That's good to hear.

Think about how Rick dealt with Peggy. He listened. He pointed out that her positive attitude might be rubbing some people the wrong way (clarification). He asked her to put herself in the position of someone who did not like something yet being *told* to like it (sharing), but he did not make a big deal out of it. He helped her to decide to try a new approach, "Perhaps if I sat down with people and went specifically over it, that might help them understand . . ." (engagement). Then he reinforced her for her good work and attitude. Peggy not only responded positively to this approach and attention, she also gained insight into her behavior and how she was affecting the other members of her team.

It is usually pleasant using the CSE Support System with people who are moving toward change already. But what about the rest of the team? What about Paul, and Judy, and, especially, what about Warren? The generic CSE Support System can be modified to fit their specific change problems. You can use very specific strategies that have been proven effective tools for helping people make the transition from endings to beginnings. They are not, however, foolproof. They are not recipes for success.

8

MOVING TOWARD BEGINNINGS: INTERVENTION STRATEGIES

*We have plenty of people in this
organization who know what to do.
The question is, will they do it?*

*Tell a man there are 300 billion stars in
the universe and he'll believe you. Tell
him a bench has wet paint and he'll
have to touch it to be sure.*

- **in•ter•vene**, *int. v.*
  To come in or between so as to modify.

To intervene is not to solve nor to take charge but, as Webster states it, to modify.

- **mod•i•fy**, *v.*
  To make less extreme, severe, or strong.

Modify is a little stronger. It carries with it the expectation of action.

Taken together, these two verbs summarize both the spirit and practice of helping people in change. *Intervene*, the intransitive verb, is the verb of showing up—taking time to talk and listen. *Modify*, the active verb, implies direction and purpose, specifically to make an erroneous attitude less extreme, severe, or strong and then, point a new way. When dealing with people who are reacting to and having problems with change, it is necessary to remember both the purpose and order of these two steps.

The CSE Support System is a general approach to helping other people move through the change process. It fulfills the needs of the verb "intervene." Its emphasis on listening and clarifying stresses that you discover rather than advocate in the initial stages of the discussion. Its focus toward the end of the process on defining action steps insures that the discussion will be more than just a polite exchange of ideas. But it does not necessarily modify. In other words, the CSE process does not—at least not directly—help make less extreme, severe, or strong the feelings associated with the other person's ending. Therefore, the CSE process needs to be supplemented with a strategy "to modify." Because there are four basic reactions to change, there will have to be four different "modify" strategies.

This chapter focuses on tailoring the CSE process to each of the four reactions: disidentification, disorientation, disengagement, and disenchantment. Think of the CSE process as the envelope and the four strategies as the potential contents of that envelope. Thus the CSE process "delivers" the correct strategy to the person with whom you are dealing.

It should be noted that the CSE process is not a lock-step process in which you do all your clarifying before you share, and all your sharing before you engage. Rather, you may find yourself clarifying, sharing, clarifying again, suggesting some possible steps, sharing a little more, and so on. To be sure, you will probably do more listening at the front end of the conversation and more engaging at the end, but the terms *clarify*, *share*, and *engage*, are descriptive rather than prescriptive. Instead of dictating the order of a series of steps, they describe activities you will use in varying combinations throughout the process.

The heart of the process is contained in the two-word strategies associated with each reaction to change.

CSE Intervention Strategies

DISORIENTATION
Explain/Plan Strategy

DISENGAGEMENT
Confront/Identify Strategy

DISENCHANTMENT
Neutralize/Acknowledge Strategy

DISIDENTIFICATION
Explore/Transfer Strategy

Although these strategies are often called "management" strategies, you do not necessarily have to be a manager to use them. Indeed, anyone can use them, as you will see later in the chapter. And although the focus in this book is the business environment and the examples in the chapter are drawn from the Averco Corporation, the skills are not limited to use within organizations. Whether dealing with people you work with, friends outside of work, or family members in change, the basic strategies apply.

DISORIENTATION: EXPLAIN/PLAN STRATEGY

People who are disoriented want information, direction, and a strategy. Without these elements, they tend to worry, maybe even project unrealistic scenarios. Judy, you may remember, in the midst of her first conversation with her co-workers, stopped at one point and said, "I don't know. Maybe I won't even *be* here in six months." Although most of her statements were factual, this one reveals the worry which is the final expression of her disorientation.

To address the needs of those who are disoriented, to "modify," or "make less severe, extreme, or strong" these individuals' sense of ambiguity, you need to *explain*. In this context, explain means more than just giving information. Information is the first step, but you also need to put that information in a framework by providing goals or a vision, a broader context to pull together the pieces of information.

At that point you can *plan* —establish a series of steps or an overall strategy.

In a changing environment, you may not be able to project the steps very far or develop a strategy in very much detail. The level of specificity, however, is not as important as the creation of order. Remember, when disorientation goes beyond being a reaction and becomes a problem, you tend to see people engaging in "Trivial Pursuit"—groping to determine the "what" instead of the "how." Explaining and planning help clarify both the what and the how.

Explain/Plan Strategy for Disoriented Individuals—Key Points

- Provide information.
- Be prepared to go into detail.
- Provide a frame: goals or an overview.
- Recognize that underneath the seemingly neutral questions, there is probably some worry.

- Provide assurances that you will take the time and effort necessary to address all concerns.
- Develop a plan or strategy—in as much detail as is realistic.
- Help the person establish priorities.

Take a look now as Rick uses the general CSE approach to conduct an Explain/Plan intervention with Judy. (This dialogue, as well as the others in this chapter, has been condensed.)

RICK: Judy, I know I've been spreading myself a little thin lately, and I may not have had the time or taken the chance to get around to you as much as I probably should have. I'm sorry. But, I'm here now. And I'll stay here until we get this thing hammered out. If we don't get it done this afternoon, then we'll make time tomorrow. Okay?

JUDY: Okay. Good. That's really what I want to hear, Rick, because I have a lot of anxiety about not having the answers I need to do my job—whatever that job turns out to be.

RICK: All right then, let's talk about those areas. But instead of me giving you a lot of information, why don't you give me your understanding of what your job will be under the new system.

JUDY: Okay. As I understand it, I'll be in charge basically of overseeing the integration of all the peripherals for Level Four mainline products and Level One mainliners—that is, the ones we're not phasing out.

RICK: Yes. We want all the peripherals to be completely integrated as the new Level Three family of products. *And,* any of those items that can also be used in Level Two—

JUDY: *New* Level Two.

RICK: Yes, *new* Level Two—all those items have to be identified as transfer/compatible.

JUDY: I'm responsible for that too?

RICK: Yes.

JUDY: Okay. That's new to me. Hmmm. Well, okay. And I'll be the one that will have to work out the new budget, personnel, and space considerations for all of them. That's what you're saying?

RICK: Correct. Are you okay with that?

JUDY: Well, yes. I mean, it's quite a job, and the incorporation of Level Two is new, but yes, okay. And Darcy Rourke, the former Level One supervisor, will be moving over as my immediate assistant.

RICK: Yes. Darcy will be your immediate assistant. In fact, she's the logical person to head up old Level One integration.

JUDY: That's right. She knows the line. Of course that makes sense. And we'll be doing a lot of the same type of duties we've been doing, but we're going to be instigating a lot of new things as well, a lot of new procedures. Is that true?

RICK: Actually, no. Eventually, yes. But for the immediate future there won't *be* any new items. Not until we get squared away at least.

JUDY: You're sure?

RICK: Judy, who can be sure of anything? But, yes. That's firm for now.

JUDY: Those are the basics then, as I see them. Is that the way you see them?

RICK: That's pretty much the way I see things. For a start. If you want to talk about more details, why don't we get into them now?

JUDY: Okay. But, it's just good to hear that that's the way things are going to be.

(Judy needed to touch the freshly painted bench)

RICK: I'm fine with that.

JUDY: Okay. Great. Now there are a lot of things I really need to get down to and get answers.

RICK: Correct me if I'm wrong, but my understanding is that your major hurdle at this point would be basically lack of specific details about basic operations—budget, staffing, workload.

JUDY: Absolutely. Now that I've got an overview, I have no problem with the changes as long as I can get the details about how it's all going to happen.

RICK: Okay, let me take the stage here and see if I can generate an overview of how I see this whole thing rolling out in the next few months. I think I can pull up an image for you. As I see it, it's kind of like a wave machine. Have you ever seen one of those? The wave goes back and forth in the tank so that at one point it's high on one end and low on the other; then it reverses, and finally it evens out. That's the way I see it here. First we're going to be overloaded for a time. We're going to have a big glut of things up front, and that's going to put a lot of pressure on you, doing two jobs. Then, when we actually physically make the change, some of the Level Four people will take some of the slack, and we may find ourselves down a little bit, but that will even out.

JUDY: So, as you see it, things are going to get very busy and hectic as we implement the integration, and then we're going to have some slack for a while, and then things will get down to a normal procedure.

RICK: Whatever "normal" is. Yes. Does that help at all?

JUDY: Yes. It does.

RICK: Okay, now, any other questions?

JUDY: There are a lot of things I need to know about sooner or later.

RICK: We can start now. If we don't finish, we'll do it tomorrow.

JUDY: That would be great. Why don't we start with a list and get things down in priority order. Then maybe you can give me some options on things I'm going to have to decide very shortly.

RICK: All right. Let's get to it.

In his meeting with Judy, Rick came prepared with all the information at his disposal and also with a sense of the whole, which he expressed in terms of analogy. Before going into the details of the change as it affected Judy, however, he made a point of assuring her that his inability to meet with her sooner was due to the press of business, and that his intention was to take as much time as they needed to meet her concerns.

Rick could have led with a lot of information, but instead he asked, "How do you see your job?" In other words, he got Judy talking. As she talked, Rick listened. He reassured her. Judy did not find out much more than she already knew, but that still helped her to feel good. She just wanted to hear it from somebody else.

In that discussion, they uncovered a few points of which Judy was unaware, and after an initial misgiving, she accepted the facts and went on.

Rick's strategy of asking instead of telling is effective. By asking the other person to lead, to express her perception, ideas, or concerns, he could move more quickly to the central issues. He saves himself the trouble of going over a lot of information which is either irrelevant or not particularly important.

Also, Rick clarified throughout the process. Because of the amount of information, it would have been very difficult for him to wait until the end and try to sum it up all at once. As you left the conversation, they were beginning to develop a list and identify priorities.

On the surface, the discussion you saw was quite simple. In it, however, Rick was able to help Judy move away from inaction toward action. Before the meeting, she had been busy, but wary. She occupied her time with "safe" tasks and postponed the key tasks because she either was not sure what to do or did not *know* what to do. Their conversation sorted these issues out and gave her a plan.

DISENGAGEMENT: CONFRONT/IDENTIFY STRATEGY

Disengaged individuals are pulling back, waiting, biding their time. They may feel that the change is a good one and are just waiting to see if they are correct, afraid to commit in case they are wrong. Or they may be disappointed or afraid, unable to get involved because they have no desire to commit. In other cases, they may just feel that the whole thing will blow over; in the meantime, they are just going to keep a low profile and hope they do not suffer too many ill effects. Finally, they may disagree with the change, but instead of fighting it, they flee.

Whatever their reasons, disengaged employees have become unhooked from the organization. Hopefully this state is temporary. Some people need time to sort out how they feel and what they want to do before committing to a change. For them, a certain amount of disengagement can be healthy. But if they remain in that state, it becomes a problem. Recall that this does not refer to the "chronically disengaged employee," but rather to one who is *newly* disengaged.

The basic strategy for dealing with disengaged people is to *confront* them with their change in behavior, and by doing that to try to draw them out and *identify* the issue so that it can be addressed.

Confrontation is a strong word, but does not necessarily need to be a strong action. To gain a better sense of what it means with the disengaged person, think of the definition of intervene: to "come in or between" and "make less extreme." There are several approaches to take:

1. *Be Direct.* If you know the person well or if he or she trusts you, you might be able to deal with the issue very simply by saying, "Bill, level with me—" or, "Ann, you're holding back. Let's talk," or, "Ed, something's eating away at you. What is it?"

2. *Provide Safety and Assurance.* Often people are quite willing to talk. They just want some assurance that it is okay or that their disclosures will not come back to haunt them. You might say, "A lot of people are having difficulties with this change. *I* am, and I sense you are too. Can we talk about it? Anything we say is just between us."

3. *Point Out Differences.* Often disengaged people are not aware of the changes in their behavior. If leveling or providing safety and assurance does not bring them out, you can simply present facts, pointing out differences in their behavior then and now or discrepancies between what they are saying and what they are doing. For example, "Phil, lately I sense that you've become a lot more

quiet and distant. I also see that you're spending a lot more time in your office. That doesn't fit the person I've come to know." Or, "I'm hearing you say 'fine, no problem,' but the look on your face and the fact that we haven't seen you around much tells me something else is going on. Anything to that?"

Usually one or some combination of these approaches will pop disengaged people out of their shell. Indeed, they may welcome the move, having wanted to talk to somebody, but feeling reluctant to do so. Once the person is willing to talk, you can proceed to identify the problem(s).

"I" Statements

A very effective technique for intervening not only with disengaged people, but anyone who is having problems with change, is the use of "I" statements. "I" statements help insure that when talking to people you focus on what "I" feel or see rather than what "you" are doing or feeling. There is a world of difference between, "I haven't seen you around lately and I miss our being able to talk," and, "You've been avoiding me lately and that doesn't make sense. You're usually so open."

The first statement is an observation; the second is a judgment. "I haven't seen you around lately" is an observed fact. "I miss our being able to talk," is an accurate statement of how "I" feel. Neither statement implies a motivation or tries to guess at "your" feelings.

The second statement, on the other hand, is replete with judgmental buzz words. "You've been spending a lot of time in your office" draws a conclusion. It interprets "haven't seen you" to mean that "you" are in avoidance. Not only are "you" avoiding, but "you" are avoiding "me." Implication: "You" ought to feel guilty—avoiding me like that.

"That doesn't make sense" is something "I" can not judge. Your behavior might make perfect sense to you. But since it does not make sense to me, I decide that, in general, it does not make sense. "You're usually so open" implies that now "you're" closed, and since open is good and closed is bad, "you" must be bad.

Such statements only serves to put people off, hurt them, and invite an argument. In general, "I" am an expert on me and "you" are an expert on you. I am an expert on what I see and what I feel, but when I try to tell you how you feel or speculate on your reasons for doing things, the communication process breaks down.

Therefore, when talking to people about their reactions to change, try to use "I" statements, not "you" statements. This advice is particularly important for disengaged people. If your objective is to draw them out, "I" statements will serve to create a sense of neutrality and, thus, make their coming out more comfortable and safe.

Confront/Identify Strategy for Disengaged People—Key Points

- Because disengaged people are pulling back, avoiding others, you will probably have to make the first move.
- To "confront" means to draw people out and help them get their feelings out on the table.
- Once people feel safe, their issues usually become clear.
- Use "I" statements, especially at the beginning of the interaction.
- When dealing with disengaged people, be prepared to dig—and listen.
- Do not expect disengaged people to suddenly become enthusiastic. Simply to move them from disengagement to a level of engagement, that is, talking and discussing, is often a gigantic leap.

What follows is a conversation between Peggy and Paul. In terms of the organizational structure, Paul is actually a little "above" Peggy, but since they both report to Rick, and because of their personal relationship, they are basically peers. Peggy, realizing that her "cheerleader" approach has been rubbing people the wrong way, has backed off. Instead, in this scene, you see her going to Paul to find out how he is doing. Listen as you see how Peggy handles it.

PAUL: Peggy? Come on in.

PEGGY: Paul. How you doing?

PAUL: Fine.

PEGGY: I haven't seen you around much.

PAUL: Yeah, I'm really busy.

PEGGY: So, everything's going smooth? No major problems?

PAUL: No, No. A lot better than the A's. They're in a real slump.

PEGGY: Paul, look. We've worked together a long time. I'm getting the sense that things *aren't* going smooth, that something's wrong. Come on, level with me.

PAUL: You're saying I'm not doing my job?

PEGGY: No, not at all. I just—

PAUL: We work. We live through it. Why does something have to be wrong?

PEGGY: Okay. "Wrong" was the wrong word. And I realize I came on a little strong. So let me put it this way. There's a big difference between what I'm hearing you say and what I'm seeing on your face, and I feel like I want to, well, talk to you about it. You're a lot more experienced than I am, and you've always helped me. Now that help isn't there, right when I need it. What I'm seeing isn't the Paul I know, that's all.

PAUL: Well, okay. I guess maybe I am a little different lately. I guess that is probably obvious. And I didn't mean to be so abrupt just then, but I *have* been here a long time. And I've been through a lot of changes, but they've never been handled like this.

PEGGY: Like what?

PAUL: It's just that there's no sense of commitment. We're just rushing into it. We're not taking time to really think things out.

PEGGY: Tell me more.

PAUL: Well, it's like this.

At this point Paul goes into a rather lengthy explanation describing the people working together all the time and how, when he first joined the company, he valued that teamwork. In his opinion, the teamwork got them through many changes. He realizes that the company is getting bigger now, but still he feels that the company is rushing headlong into the unknown.

PEGGY: Thanks for talking to me, Paul. And at the risk of oversimplifying, tell me if I'm wrong, but what I sense is that you've lost a sense of where the company's going and whether you can keep pace, and also that the teamwork that could help us keep pace is missing.

PAUL: It's just not the way we should do things. It's like going back to my home town and not recognizing the streets or the trees or even my house.

PEGGY: What do you think you want to see?

PAUL: I know we can't stand still. But when this company was founded, we worked things out before we launched into things. Everybody was coming together toward one thing. But even in our group we don't have that sense of wanting to get together and find out the best way to be able to do this, so that nobody gets lost in the shuffle.

PEGGY: All right. I don't want to sound Polyanna, but I think maybe we *can* do that. Can I explain what *I* see?

PAUL: Sure.

PEGGY: I think this new system will give us a *greater* sense of unity, if for no other reason than we'll all be working under the same roof. And with One and Four being combined, we don't have a choice. We're *all* starting over. We're going to *have* to work together and help each other learn. It's as simple as that. Now, am I laying it on too thick?

PAUL: No. Maybe you're right.

PEGGY: I feel I am. But maybe that's just me.

PAUL: (Smiles) Might be.

PEGGY: But I do see us coming together. You're right about the way it's been. Everybody running around with blinders on, scared to death they'll lose their jobs. We've never experienced that before, right?

PAUL: That's right. We've never laid people off before.

PEGGY: So, all of us are a little nervous about our jobs. That's natural. That's why we have to pull together.

PAUL: Yeah.

PEGGY: But now we *are* pulling together a little more, and the one person we all figured would really be there with us—you—is gone.

PAUL: Um hum.

PEGGY: So what I'm here for is to say, we miss your presence. It's as simple as that. Am I being too gushy?

PAUL: No. Not at all, Peggy, and I don't mean to be so stonefaced. I'm just thinking.

PEGGY: Well, I've said enough as it is. I'll just let you think. But you'll give the new team here the benefit of the doubt?

PAUL: I'll give it the benefit of the doubt. I guess that's only fair.

PEGGY: Thanks, Paul. Talk to you later.

PAUL: Yeah.

Initially, Peggy was met by Paul's "no problem" facade. (He may also have been bracing himself for another onslaught of Peggy's perkiness.) Peggy was sensitive, however, and by using "I" statements she was able to bring Paul out. He resisted at first, but gradually the comfort and trust levels rose. As Paul talked, his real concerns became clear. In this process, Peggy made a classic clarification "At the risk of oversimplifying, let me see if I've got this. . . ." At this point, Peggy has identified Paul's real concern, or at least one of them. Now the question is, "So what?" Paul has disclosed a problem, but Peggy is not really in a position to do anything about it. So what good did it do?

In general, simply talking can do a lot of good. It can start movement. Paul is a little closer to accepting and working with the change now than he was when they began. Granted, Paul is not enthusiastic, but his willingness to take a second look or give the change the benefit of the doubt is, for him, a rather large leap. Peggy's action serves as a simple example for what can be a very powerful force in a changing organization: increased employee-to-employee communication.

DISENCHANTMENT: NEUTRALIZE/ ACKNOWLEDGE STRATEGY

People who are disenchanted need to move through their anger. They are reacting to a loss, and unless they have the opportunity to vent, this anger will only build up, increase the blockage, and spill over into other forms of negative behavior.

Disenchantment can be overt and loud or it can be a more subdued, smoldering anger. In both cases, the reaction is not hard to identify because it is highly charged. Even people who attempt to hide their anger or feel it would be politically unwise to get mad will have difficulty. The reaction will show in their body language, tone of voice, and in their actions.

Since it is nearly impossible to reason or talk with a person feeling this way, the first step in the intervention process is *neutralize*—bring the person from a highly charged state to neutral.

"Neutralize" here is not used in the negative sense of demeaning or dismissing the person's reaction. Rather it is used in the sense of letting the fizz out of the bottle. The best way to do that is to provide a safe environment and allow the person to vent.

Once people have let it all out, it is common for them to suddenly realize what they have done and feel embarrassed. They say things like, "I really made a fool out of myself, didn't I?" Or, "I didn't realize how strongly I felt about that."

You have probably had the experience of being near a power lawnmower or chainsaw or some other loud, constant noise. You grow accustomed to it, accept it as "normal." Then, when it suddenly stops, you are struck with how quiet it is, and you realize how draining the noise had been all along. The process of venting is like turning off the noise. The disenchanted person will probably be struck with how irritating they had been both to themselves and to others.

Because of this realization, it is also important to *acknowledge* the person. Let them know that you do not hold their anger against them and that they need not be embarrassed.

Acknowledge that it is *normal*. "Don't worry about it. I'd feel the same way. I blow up sometimes, too. It's a normal way to feel."

Neutralize/Acknowledge Strategy for Disenchanted Individuals—Key Points

- Disenchantment usually manifests itself in the form of anger.
- The first step is to let the employees "vent"—get the feelings out in the open.
- To neutralize does not mean to stop or deny angry feelings; rather it means to allow the person to move through the feelings and expel the blockage.
- To acknowledge does not necessarily mean to agree, but simply to say, in effect, "It's okay to be angry," or, "That's a valid concern," or, "I understand your reason for being upset."

Consider how Rick handles Warren's disenchantment. He has asked Warren to stop by his office.

RICK: Come on in, Warren.

WARREN: (Sarcastically) You rang?

RICK: You still upset?

WARREN: Yes, I *am still* upset.

RICK: Okay. Let's talk about it. Let it out. What's bugging you?

WARREN: You really want it?

RICK: Both barrels.

WARREN: You may not like what I've got to say.

RICK: I'll like it less if you *don't* tell me. And nothing goes outside this office. So try me.

WARREN: Okay. Well, first of all, the changeover is so
           messed up because I am spending so much
           time on the new system right now that there's
           no one to handle the problems with the old
           system. I mean we can't do *two* jobs; there's
           not enough time in the day to get all the
           things done around here. I don't know what
           anyone was thinking about when they plan-
           ned this stupid thing. So that's that. More im-
           portant, I don't know what the priorities are
           in this system. I don't know where to begin. I
           ask you, has anyone given any thought to the
           amount of paperwork we're going to be de-
           veloping with all these new reports? I mean,
           we have never, ever had such a bureaucratic
           mess like this. It's crazy and nobody seems to
           care. We're blitzed with work, and they in-
           vent new forms. Who thought of that? And
           I'll tell you what bothers me the most; that's
           the fact that they're just arbitrarily throwing
           out all the work *I* did on the old system. I
           mean, it took me long enough to put that to-
           gether, and I don't think anybody understood
           it any better than I do, but I did, and I know it
           worked. We finally got all the bugs and prob-
           lems out of it. Now that's totally gone. People
           come to me with questions now, and I don't
           have any of the answers. People used to trust
           me. They came to me because I was an au-
           thority, and now you know what you've done
           to me? I mean, you've eroded all the confi-
           dence in me. That's not a very efficient way
           to run a company. Taking someone in a posi-
           tion of authority and cutting them off at the
           knees.

Warren continues in this vein for a while, basically expanding on his main issues. Finally, he runs out of steam.

RICK: More?
WARREN: You're saying that's not enough for you?
RICK: No. That's plenty. Just checking.
WARREN: I'm done.

RICK: You're sure.

WARREN: Yeah.

RICK: Want to go get the C.E.O.? Bring him down here and we'll beat his brains out?

WARREN: Come on.

RICK: Okay, let me summarize this—for both you and me. As I heard it, there are four major areas you're concerned about. You're concerned about losing productivity; you're talking about the priorities and the lines of communication; you're talking about the unmanageable papertrail; and you're talking about the fact that you can't answer people's questions when they come to you. Right?

WARREN: Yes. When you put it that way, those are the basics. I thought there were more issues, but—yeah, those are the issues. And maybe I came on a little too strong, too. I can get really worked up about things, and—

RICK: Don't apologize. I understand why you're angry. I'd blow up too if I were in that kind of situation. It's really come down on you more than a lot of other people. Now, in terms of these issues, it seems that in any new system, in any corporation, those first problems—productivity, priorities, and communication—are going to be there.

WARREN: Okay. I can accept that. I don't like it, but I can accept it. But that doesn't address the last part of the problem, which I think is the most important. People no longer view me as an expert because I can't answer their questions.

RICK: You're saying you can accept the confusion and hassle, but when leadership is, like you said, cut off at the knees, *that's* serious.

WARREN: Exactly! I'm a lame duck to those people.

RICK: Okay. That gives me a better sense of what's going on here. So, let me ask you this. There are some things that I think I do real well. Why are you good at what you do?

In this exchange, Rick let Warren vent to bring himself to neutrality. Rick listened as Warren just kept talking until he was through. Then Rick acknowledged Warren and narrowed down what seemed an encyclopedia of information to four points. This lack of focus on the underlying problems is a common occurrence with people when they are blowing off a lot of energy. It may have seemed like there were "100 problems," but really they have 25 examples each of four problems. That is what happened with Warren. When Rick ticked them off, Warren was a little surprised, but he had to agree, "Yes, I guess you're right. I guess there were only four."

Compare this encounter with Rick's mini-clarifications with Judy. The clarification in both instances is present, but quite different.

Rick next legitimized Warren's anger. He basically acknowledged, "Yes, it's come down on you." He identified with him, "I understand your reasons for being upset. I'd blow up, too."

By allowing Warren to work through his disenchantment, Rick cleared the way for dealing with Warren's core problem, disidentification.

DISIDENTIFICATION: EXPLORE/ TRANSFER STRATEGY

Disidentified people feel that the rug has been pulled out from under them. They are experiencing loss because something or somebody they identified with has been taken away from them. It may be a job, a competency, a position, a team, a location, a boss, a career path, even a machine.

Whatever it was, they found comfort and security in it. The loss can run the gamut from eliminating a job function, to introducing a new computer system, to losing a team member through promotion, to getting paid on the 5th and 25th instead of on the 15th and the 30th, to, as was the case in one company, replacing Pepsi Light with Mellow Yellow in a soda vending machine. The reaction to this loss can be quite strong, which is why it is common for disidentification to occur simultaneously with disenchantment.

Bridges uses the realization that there is no Santa Claus as a classic example of disenchantment. It could also serve as an example of disidentification. Some children accept and work through that realization more quickly than others. They have moved on to new beginnings and feel duty bound to break the bad news to other kids. The response they get is often anger, denial, and hurt. Indeed, some children go on believing in Santa Claus long after they are "supposed to."

Parents often credit this extended belief to the child's not wanting to give up a source of gifts, but it goes deeper than that. Santa is not only a source of gifts, but also a symbol of kindness, caring, and magic—of childhood. True disidentification goes beyond the loss of an outward thing or person or place; it is the loss of a perceived way of life.

Because of this attachment, disidentification in organizations is also often accompanied by rigidity—a strong attachment to form and a martyr's sense of victimization. People will defend to the hilt some obviously outmoded form, claiming that it would be criminal to lose it. They phrase their objections in logical, technical language, but the real attachment is emotional. The trouble is, problematically disidentified people can not see the difference.

You may recall that disidentified people make statements in two parts. Before the comma they are true; after the comma they are false. "I used to work with these people but now I don't have any friends." "I used to be really competent in my job but now you might as well fire me." That is why disidentification is so difficult to deal with. When somebody says, "Well I used to belong to a group, and now nobody likes me anymore," you may say, "No, that's not true." Then they will come back with, "What do you mean? You're saying I still belong to that group?" It is difficult to deal with disidentified people, because if you address the irrational part, they will come back and hit you with the rational part.

For these reasons, dealing with the disidentified person can be very demanding. Telling or reasoning usually will produce only an unwinnable argument. Therefore, it is necessary to help them discover the difference between truth and falsity or the distinction between that which is a reasonable argument and that which is unreasonable and receives its power from raw emotion alone.

The key verbs in the disidentification strategy are *explore* and *transfer:* To come up with some possible ideas and then implement the ideas to form a bridge or link to the new system. It sounds easy. "Feeling the loss of your team?" you say. "No problem. There are some new teams forming. We'll get you in one you like and you'll have a new set of friends in no time."

However reasonable this argument is, *telling* it to the disidentified person does not usually work. You can not explore the issue *for* them. They need to explore it for themselves. The object of the explore process is *to separate the emotion from the form.* To enable this process:

1. *Involve them in a discussion* of what they liked or valued in the "old way." Some people argue that to do this is not effective, that it only allows the person to dwell on the past and wallow in negative emotions. On the contrary, by talking about the sense of loss, the person is more likely to identify what was most important to him or her in the old system. It may be a sense of belonging, a feeling of being known, familiarity with a product, or a sense of knowing what was expected.

Like the overall outcome of the self-management process, this discussion will begin to translate anxiety into fear. Specifically, it will begin to link emotions to forms, and, most importantly, tacitly establish the possibility that if the emotion and the form can be separated, maybe it is possible for a new form to generate the same emotion.

That moves you to the second step of exploration:

2. Ask, "How can we get you what you value in the new system?" Maybe they will say, "We can't," and fall back into disidentification. But if they have separated the emotion from the form, they may see possibilities.

For example, the statement, "I'm comfortable with this keyboard. I don't want to use the new one," may become, "I learned to be comfortable with this keyboard, maybe I can learn to be comfortable with the new one." Or, "We started this company with a commitment to help people solve financial problems. But now, if we're just going to hawk products and throw away our consulting function, just because of competition and the need to make a buck, well, I don't want any part of it!" This may become, "What I really valued in my job was meeting people and helping them. In this new market, we can't afford that kind of one-on-one service. It eats up too much time. But there may be ways to still meet people and help them, not so much through individual consultation, but more through creative combinations of various financial products."

In both cases, the old forms (a keyboard and individual consultation) were tied to emotions (comfort and satisfaction in helping people); and, in the minds of the two people, the form and the emotion were inseparable. But when you separate the emotion from the form, possibilities present themselves.

Once you help disidentified people break through the emotion/form dilemma, you can begin the *transfer* process. Simply stated, to "transfer" is to flesh out the ideas in concrete definable steps. In this sense "transfer" and the "engage" step of CSE are virtually the same.

Explore/Transfer Strategy for Disidentified Individuals—Key Points

- Disidentified people tend to identify strongly not only to a particular form, but to a way of life and to the emotions that way of life engendered.
- Disenchantment often accompanies disidentification.
- To "explore" is to help the person see that form and emotion are separable.
- Questions work better than statements in the process of exploration.

Let's see how Rick continued with his conversation with Warren once he discovered that Warren's primary change problem was one of disidentification.

RICK: Let me ask you this. There're some things that I think I do real well. Why are you good at what you do?

WARREN: Well, I don't know. I never thought about it. But, okay, I pick up on things I guess. I'm a fast learner. And I have some experience to draw on. And I think I know how to get things done. I think you'd call me a resourceful person. And I'm good with people. I think I get good work from people. If *I* know what's going on, I'm a good teacher. I know how to explain things.

RICK: Exactly. And that's precisely the point. That's why I want you to be the lead person in the new area in this new system. Because you're good at it. You know that. I know that. The company knows that. In the past, when somebody came to you—Boom—you had it. Right there. When this new system is up and running, who do you think will learn it first? And who do you think the people are going to come to with their questions? When you get up to speed on this, who do you think all the people are going to come to? That's you. People have confidence in you, and that's who they're going to come to.

WARREN: But I don't know the system!

RICK: Who does?! But you just told me you were a quick study, right?

WARREN: Right.

RICK: So you'll be the first to learn it, right?

WARREN: I guess so.

RICK: And then you can work the way you did before.

WARREN: Yeah, but *until* then, it's going to be chaotic.

RICK: You're right. It is. But you can master the new system the same way you mastered the old one. So let's you and me sit down and try to iron out some of the ways that we can push this process along and make it work.

WARREN: Well, okay. If that's the way it's gotta be, then I guess we're just going to have to gut it out. It is *we* isn't it?

RICK: Huh?

WARREN: It is *we*. I am going to be reporting to you still,
           aren't I?

RICK: Me? Of course. Why do you—Oh! You
           thought you might be moved under John?

WARREN: Anything's possible in this mess.

RICK: Are you kidding? You'd burn John out in a
           week. Just when we need him most. (Both
           laugh) No, seriously. The two of us and the
           team, we're staying intact.

WARREN: Well, I have to tell you, that makes me feel a
           whole lot better.

RICK: That goes both ways, Warren. So let's start by
           getting—

In this interchange, Rick used an interrogatory approach, as
he did with Judy. Rather than telling him, he asked Warren,
"What are you good at?" That tactic got Warren off the defensive, because now he had to talk about what he is good at. It
took him a while to shift mentally. "Well, I never thought
about it . . ." he said, and then it finally clicked in. He started
to talk about what he was doing. In effect, what he was doing
was *explore*. By talking about what he was good at, Warren
began to separate emotions from forms. The confidence people had in him, his desire to teach people and be the expert
had all been attached in Warren's mind to a form—the old
system. When he saw that he could gain these same things in
the new system, he was ready to work out the transfer. Instead
of dwelling on what he had lost, Warren began to recognize
the generic skills he had, even though he was not consciously
aware that that was what he was doing. "The explore" strategy
shattered the shell Warren was in. It got him to the point
where he could see the connection or the "transfer," the bridge
to the new area.

Then Rick explained the new system in very honest terms.
"All right, you're no different than anybody else. Nobody
knows. But you just told me you were a quick study. So who's
going to be the first one to learn it? And who did people come
to anyway? You know, give me a break, Warren."

Warren raised some objections, but basically saw the logic of it. He played fair in the sense of saying, "Okay, I see your point here." Rick was very honest. It was not going to be easy. And he saw the transfer and how to make it.

Then right at the end, a surprise! A revelation of Warren's identification with Rick and his department. Rick is not only Warren's boss, but his friend. Perhaps the prospect of Rick, his friend, possibly letting him go, perhaps to report to John was at the deepest level, the source of a lot of Warren's anger.

IN SUMMARY

The intervention strategies are summarized below:

DISORIENTATION
Explain/Plan Strategy

DISENGAGEMENT
Confront/Identify Strategy

DISENCHANTMENT
Neutralize/Acknowledge Strategy

DISIDENTIFICATION
Explore/Transfer Strategy

These strategies have much in common, but they also differ in certain key respects. Moreover, it is the differences, not the similarities that have the most significance. The differences underscore the importance of dealing with and meeting the needs of *individuals* within the work unit. A "vanilla" approach simply will not work.

You now understand how people respond in change situations and why they may have difficulty dealing with change. You know how to recognize and diagnose the four reactions to change and have specific strategies to deal with these reactions—that is, you have the skills and strategies needed to help those with whom you work move through the transitions stage.

It is important to realize, however, that the success of these strategies usually depends on one key factor: your attitude.

If *you* do not believe in the change, if you feel more like a victim than an owner of change, the strategies will probably not succeed. In short, you cannot give away what you do not have. Thus the success of your attempts to help others move to new beginnings depends on your ability to be truly committed yourself.

A FINAL NOTE: KNOWING VERSUS DOING

Many of the specific skills that will help you effectively deal with a changing environment may already be familiar to you. If you are like many people, however, you may seldom use these skills. Why? Most of the skills are relatively simple to understand, but not necessarily easy to do. To examine this distinction more fully, pair the words "simple" and "easy" with their respective opposites, "complex" and "difficult."

Simple   Easy

Complex   Difficult

Think for a moment about these two pairs of words. How would you characterize the differences between them? Some of the most commonly given distinctions are summarized below:

Simple/Complex	Easy/Difficult
Knowing	Doing
Intellectual	Emotional/physical
Theoretical	Hands-on
Thinking	Acting
Abstract	Practical

As they stand, the words and their descriptors form the skeleton for an explanation of how people learn—or fail to learn.

The first step in learning is translating something complex into something simple. It is an intellectual process.

High schools and colleges approach learning largely along this line. For example, when you begin to learn geography, biology, English, or management—you tend to approach it first from an intellectual point of view, taking a complex body of information and making it, if not simple, at least simpler. You divide the subject into parts, make distinctions, identify steps, and then test yourself.

Now a question arises, "If you understand something, does that mean you can do it?" In other words, if it is simple to understand, does that make it easy? Can you make this jump?

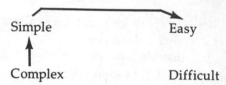

The answer is clearly no. But unfortunately our educational systems tacitly reinforce the misconception that you can jump from simple to easy. This erroneous assumption can be detected in statements often made by people starting a new job, "I can't do this; I must be stupid." Or, "I can't do this; I must not have learned it very well." Such statements indicate that many times people equate understanding with mastery.

The ability to stop smoking illustrates the point. How complex is it to understand that smoking is bad for your health and that you should not smoke? Certainly, it is not very complex; it is quite simple. How easy is it for a smoker to stop smoking? Not very easy; it is, in fact, quite difficult.

Or take skiing. Anyone who skis knows that you cannot go from intellectual mastery, that is, reading a book about skiing, to actual mastery on the slopes.

**Just understanding something does not
necessarily mean you can do it.**

Knowing and *doing* involve two separate sets of skills, one intellectual and the other emotional.

Thus learning does not proceed from complex to simple to easy; rather, it proceeds from complex to simple to difficult to easy in an N progression:

Step 1: Complex to Simple. You take a body of knowledge and break it into its component parts to intellectually understand it.

Step 2: Simple to Difficult. In applying the knowledge, you move from the comfort of knowing to the discomfort of making mistakes.

Step 3: Difficult to Easy. Through practice, you make the task if not easy, at least less difficult to do.

The key step in the learning process is Step 2, going from simple to difficult. At first this step seems like a step backward. You may find yourself struggling and confused by a process or concept that seemed so clear and simple. You may even experience a drop in productivity.

If you have held a golf club a certain way for twenty years and somebody shows you a new and better way to hold it, your game will probably get worse before it gets better. Similarly, if you have dealt with people in a certain way for years, trying a new way of dealing with them will at first be confusing and frustrating. This period of adjustment requires you to "destruct to reconstruct."

It takes courage to voluntarily take this dip. But in the long run, it pays off in better performance and a sense of accomplishment.

The concepts and strategies presented in this chapter make sense logically. They are simple to understand. But in practice, they will not be easy—at least not at first. The challenge to you is to apply the skills that have been "simplified." The actual application of the skills depends on your commitment to begin by first enduring the discomfort of "difficult" and then working toward "easy."

9

BEGINNINGS: BUYING INTO THE CHANGE TOGETHER

To deal with the change, I committed us to try certain things, with the understanding that they might not all work. Later, I realized that what I started there—even though I didn't see it at the time—was to create two things: an action plan and trust. The action plan had varying degrees of success and failure. But the trust was always there. If we didn't have that trust, we would have complained ourselves out of existence a long time ago.

After enlightenment—the laundry.
Zen saying.

Endings and transitions differ from person to person; beginnings tend to be shared. The process of working through an ending and moving into the transition stage is generally an individual activity. To be sure, you will probably have help in this process, but the issues to be worked out are personal. Once movement along the Change Response Scale has begun, however, you will tend to come into closer proximity with other people heading toward the same goal.

The overall goal or outcome of the organization—when effectively articulated—serves as a point on the horizon. As the individuals move closer to it, their paths begin to converge. The issues of individual adjustment gradually give way to the desire for an effective and shared transformation of the organizational culture. For this reason, the one-on-one skills of endings and transitions gradually give way to group skills.

This chapter focuses on some of the skills and practices of this final stage in the change process. The focus question for this phase of growth is:

How do we gain commitment to the change?

Just because people are moving in the same direction, toward the same goal, does not necessarily mean that they are committed to it. Indeed, if their endings have included anger, resentment, a sense of betrayal, or a feeling of being ignored, their commitment will probably have to be earned, their trust restored. The good news is that a small core of people is probably ready to help restore these vital elements and that may be enough. According to Harold Willins' *The Trim Tab Factor*, a relatively small percentage of a total group can make a significant change in the culture of that group. As Willins suggests, for example, it would require the commitment of only 20 percent of the population to eliminate nuclear war.

Also, people buy in for different reasons, depending on where they are in the Growth Curve. For companies in Phase I, one critical issue is entrepreneurism and risk taking. Employees feel they are stakeholders because if they succeed, they all succeed; if they fail, they all fail. Commitment is more or less a given.

In Phase II, however, most of this feeling is lost. In this phase, people have moved from the visionary "what if" to a reliance on efficiency and the management of routine. Buy-in is not really an issue. The system is running smoothly. If you are doing your job, commitment is assumed. It does not take any effort. Commitment is no longer a group covenant to pull together and make something work; rather it is loyalty to a system that *does* work. Often people in Phase II organizations tend to forget what commitment really is. As a result, when the organization moves into Phase III, they have forgotten one of the things they need most to make it through the difficulties of early Phase III.

In fact, the strategies of beginnings look very much like the strategies for Phase I. This time, instead of supporting the lone entrepreneur, you want to create what might be called a "team entrepreneur." What is needed is not an individual Lone Ranger or a single visionary, but a group of people with a common purpose, a common vision. Leadership skills supersede management skills, and the focus needs to be on building high-performance teams within the organization and on getting those teams pulling in the same direction. One way organizations often attempt to do this is through symbols or ceremonies.

SYMBOLS AND CEREMONIES

After a change has taken place, companies tend to symbolically end and begin; that is, they have some symbolic activity—an "event"—such as a picnic or banquet or retreat to mark the start of the beginning. Often they develop a special symbol to commemorate the new beginning. It might be a new mission statement, banners around the office, or a new logo—something visible.

Several months after its integration of Levels One and Four, Averco management *thought* it was over the hump and at the point of beginnings. They wanted a symbol, a ceremony to cut the old and begin the new; so, they planned "Averco Day." It was an Outward-Bound type experience for the purpose of team building and to symbolically shed the old ways and move on to the new. Averco called off business for a day, and the staff went out to a natural area where there was a tree and rope course set up. People joined up in teams, with management and employees spread evenly. They did not compete against each other, but against themselves. This was followed by a picnic where everyone had a terrific time. People came back to work feeling very good about the event. The intent was to end all the hard times that had gone before and to symbolize the rebirth of the company through a group activity. By calling off business for an entire day, the company had made a sacrifice in a genuine effort to show the employees that they cared about them.

Did Averco Day succeed as a beginning in which people were able to forget the past? The answer is no. Just because they had a day to go out and have fun together did not mean that everybody had moved up to 8 or 9 on the Change Response Scale. If you had taken a score at that point, you probably would have found that they were still all over the scale, with arrows going back and forth. In fact, one of the most commonly heard statements about the day was like this one, "I thought it was a *very* successful day, and the thing I liked best was being able to meet people I'd never met before, or never really known, and finding out that they were going through a lot of the same things I was." Thus the value for this person and many like her was the ability to share experiences, to understand the change, and to get ideas.

Following Averco Day, management decided to set up subsequent meetings for the teams to get together to work on how the new system was going to function. Instead, in those meetings people talked about the issues they were facing. They talked about things that were still unresolved in their minds. They talked about their gripes. It turned out that what were intended to be "beginnings" groups were actually "endings/transitions" groups. Averco saw that the groups had not gotten fully onto beginnings yet, even though that was the intent. Management had jumped to beginnings before people were really at the beginnings stage. The employees, however, were not yet ready to get together to chart the future course of the company. There was still a lot of excess baggage and unfinished business. The groups that were set up to chart the company's future were actually dealing with those unfinished issues.

At this point the company could have insisted, "We don't have any problems anymore. You've got to talk about the beginnings." Or it could let it go in the direction it was obviously going, recognizing the unfinished business, and using the groups as support groups to help people move through. That is what they chose to do. Many of the groups used their time to mourn the past, work on transitions, and clarify the future.

One important lesson to be learned from the Averco experience is that, although the ceremony in this case was not the beginning of beginnings, it *was* the end of endings. After that day, the company began to move more quickly through the change process. People still remember that event, Averco Day, as one way the company was able to demonstrate its commitment to helping them work through the change process. What may have begun for the wrong reasons, as an attempt to push people to beginnings, ended up positively because it served to symbolize intent and to give permission to grieve.

Symbols work best when they are allowed to change and evolve and when they encourage participation. Therefore symbols such as posters or slogans tend to be static and cosmetic. They are generally the attempt of upper management (or worse, the public relations department) to instill confidence or motivate. Because they tend to come from the top down, they are seldom more than decoration. If, however, employees are allowed to participate in the process of creating a symbol or slogan, if they are allowed to "own" it, the chances for success are greater.

Generally, effective symbols tend to be spontaneous. For example, one company had the "pink slip" award. Many people were worried about getting fired—getting "the pink slip" was the phrase commonly used, even though it was not literally true. Then one department decided to take the idea of the pink slip and turn it into a positive as opposed to a negative.

Somebody wrote somebody else a positive, reinforcing statement on a pink paper. The person receiving it was delighted at
the complimentary message it contained. Giving and getting
pink slips quickly became a tradition within the company.
When people had good ideas, they wrote them on a pink slip.
They turned a negative into a positive.

The best symbols tend to bubble up from the organization.
Thus the trick in the beginnings stage is not to create symbols
as much as it is to allow them to surface and recognize them
when they do. Note also that spontaneous symbols tend very
often to be unorthodox and even a little threatening as opposed to the "ideologically pure" slogans generated by upper
management. For example, the pink slip award borders on
irreverence, yet proved to be a very powerful force in the
organization.

People are born symbol makers. If this tendency is stifled,
they will generate negative symbols. If this tendency is encouraged, they will generate symbols which, if not totally positive in the sense of unreservedly embracing a change, will at
least be powerful in expressing the desire for movement toward that change.

SYMBOLS AND VALUES

The one constant in change should be an organization's value
system. If, along with the change, there is a contradiction in
values, the chance for the organization to move on to new
beginnings is greatly reduced. A strong value system acts as a
constant to support the movement from endings through transitions to new beginnings. The value system acts as a thread of
purpose keeping the constantly changing forms in some kind
of alignment.

Values are often embodied in symbols, but if the symbol
contradicts the value, its effect is lost. In one case, for example,
a company decided to signify its change from authoritative to
participative management by eliminating company cars and
reserved parking places because typically only those in upper
management had them. This move was a strong, positive symbol of a new value, until it was learned that the president of
the company still had a company car and reserved parking

place. This single exception ruined the symbol and discredited the value.

Consequently, during change, the personal symbolism of an organization's leadership is key. What tend to be noticed and remembered are not so much the management skills, but symbolic acts. If, for instance, a new policy is instituted as part of a change, and then the informal system sees someone in upper management contradict that policy, it is unlikely they will commit to the change. It is more likely they will use the contradiction to fuel disenchantment.

Consider the example of the company that hired a new human resources development head during a period of downsizing. The reason given for the downsizing was cost reduction. This new human resources development person's first act was to refurnish her office in an opulent manner. Her intent was to create an office "unlike other offices in the building" that would allow people to relax and feel more at ease. Despite her good intentions, that act finished her. No one believed the reason for the downsizing was cost, and no one remained committed to cutting costs. Her well-intentioned act created subtle resentment as well as numerous negative, and often very humorous, symbols that far outweighed all the positive efforts she made to help employees.

That *everyone* align themselves with the organization's purpose is critical. Upper management, especially, must be sensitive to contradicting in any way the beliefs and vision they have set forth. The informal system will be looking for such a contradiction which would give them valid reasons to hang on to the past as well as ammunition to attack the new beginning.

Ideally, the value system is put into writing. An example of one such value system is that of Cray Research. It is important to note, however, that it is an evolving statement that has been revised once and may be again from time to time, in keeping with the Cray philosophy.

THE CRAY STYLE*

At Cray Research, we take what we do very seriously; but we don't take ourselves too seriously.

*Reprinted by permission of Cray Research, Inc.

There is a sense of pride at Cray. Professionalism is important. People are treated like and act like professionals. But people are professional without being stuffy.

Cray people trust each other to do their jobs well and with the highest ethical standards. We take each other very seriously.

We have a strong sense of quality—quality in our products and services, of course; but also quality in our working environment, in the people we work with, in the tools that we use to do our work, and in the components we choose to make what we make.

Economy comes from high value, not from low cost. Aesthetics are part of quality. The effort to create quality extends to the communities in which we work and live as well.

The Cray approach is informal and nonbureaucratic. Verbal communication is key, not memos. "Call, don't write" is the watchword.

People are accessible at all levels.

People also have fun working at Cray Research. There is laughing in the halls, as well as serious conversation. More than anything else, the organization is personable and approachable; but still dedicated to getting the job done.

With informality, however, there is also a sense of confidence. Cray people feel like they are on the winning side. They feel successful, and they are. It is this sense of confidence that generates the attitude of "go ahead and try it, we'll make it work."

Cray people like taking responsibility for what they do and thinking for themselves. At the same time, they are proud to share a single mission—making the world's fastest computers.

Because the individual is key at Cray, there is a real diversity in the view of what Cray Research really is. In fact, Cray Research is many things to many people. The consistency comes in providing these diverse people with the opportunity to fulfill themselves and experience achievement.

The creativity, then, that emerges from the company comes from the many ideas of the individuals who are here. And that is the real strength of Cray Research.

Cray's statement is both effective and risky. It contains "nice" words such as "personable," "approachable," "creativity," and "fun." It also presents a compelling vision for an organization working together. The key to living up to this organization's mission will rest with Cray's managers and employees. If their behavior demonstrates a commitment to fulfilling the promises of the statement, the results will be powerful. If their behavior contradicts the statement, the intent of the statement could turn against itself. That is the risk, but taking such a risk is exactly what is needed during change.

If you are reaffirming old values or creating new ones, people need to know it. They need to see it—in writing and in action.

"What if we can't live up to such an idea?" someone may ask. The question expresses a fear that we can not risk committing to something we might not be able to live up to. True, as you saw in the case of the opulent office, a single act can undermine a positive intent. In general, however, people will tolerate exceptions as long as people are able to follow through on promises, to admit failure, and to attempt rectification when they start up again. As one person at Averco described it, "To deal with the change, I committed us to try certain things, with the understanding that they might not all work. Later, I realized that what I started there—even though I didn't see it at the time—was to create two things: an action plan and trust. The action plan had varying degrees of success and failure. But the trust was always there. If we didn't have that trust, we would have complained ourselves out of existence a long time ago."

ACTIVITIES OF BEGINNINGS

Having looked at the symbols and ceremonies commonly associated with beginnings and with the need for maintaining a constant value system during change, turn your attention now to the more tactical aspects of new beginnings: planning, goal setting, long- and short-term strategies, and implementation procedures. As a rule, companies are fairly good at such activities. But over and above these matters are some broader questions. How can you truly see what the results of a change will be? How do you communicate to others in a way that gets them to identify with the change? How can you realistically get yourself and those with whom you work committed to the changes?

To begin, consider these questions, "What are the activities of beginnings? What do people typically do when a new project starts?" Generally the activities of beginnings are planning, training, communicating, establishing procedures, assigning duties, establishing controls, developing benchmarks, getting input, monitoring, adjusting, restructuring, focusing, scheduling meetings, setting deadlines, budgeting, gathering resources, and the like. All these activities could be summarized under the general category of *A PLAN*. And everyone agrees that plans are critical to success.

Now take another word: *Vision*. When you hear the word *vision*, what comes to mind? Distance, wholeness, ideal, color, big picture, spectrum, projection, inspiration, height, future, picture, fantasy, mind's eye, trial and error, make believe, hope, imagination, etc.

Compare this list with the words associated with *plan*. You should note two basic differences or "themes."

1. The *plan* list has more to do with details and actual steps to take. It tends to be concrete, rigid, hard, focused on today.
2. The *vision* list is more general, but also more inspiring and easier to identify with. It tends to be abstract, open, flexible, and focused on the future.

VISIONS AND PLANS

Visions and plans are mutually dependent. One can not exist without the other. A vision without a plan is just somebody's dream. A plan without a vision is blind activity. You need both. In terms of time, vision comes first, the plan follows. Visions draw you; plans push you. So, obviously, it is good to have a vision. Very few people disagree. Consequently, companies spend a lot of time developing mission statements. In spite of that investment, good visions tend to be few and far between. Why does that happen?

Have you ever had this situation? A manager says, "Here's my vision," and then he gives you a plan. In other words, the manager is saying, in effect, "Here's my dream. I want you to be involved in it and, by the way, I've worked out all the details, so just *do* it." Are you being drawn or pushed in that situation? Obviously, you are being pushed.

Clearly, disguising a plan as a vision is the wrong thing to do. Then why do managers do it? The primary reason is that many managers are still caught up in some or all of the following demands.

1. *Time.* It is easier to lay out a plan for people. It is more efficient. You can sit in your office and work the whole thing out and not have to take up a lot of other people's time and energy. This tendency is doubled in the case of a change. Everybody is overburdened as it is. So at the very point where you need a good vision, you have the least receptive culture to create one.

2. *Lack of confidence in other people.* Very often managers believe they must be responsible for all major decisions. They do not trust the capabilities of their people. They devalue their employees' ability to contribute, believing that no one employee could develop the whole plan. That is true. The manager is probably the best person to develop the big picture, but as a group the employees can provide tremendous input, experience, and commitment.

3. *Control.* Many managers simply do not want to give up control. They see it as giving away a very key part of their authority. To give up control is to deny the need for managers. The result is that, by keeping what they consider to be "their" control, managers actually lose control because they become stressed and overburdened and subsequently function inefficiently.

4. *The need to remain "business-like."* Many managers do not want to promote something as vague as a vision. Vision, to many, sounds spiritual or existential—and that is scary. Even the word seems soft. They need hard facts. Also, their superiors judge them in terms of how specific their plans are. The work culture punishes activity that is not worked out in detail.

These are all very strong cultural influences that tend to squash what everybody agrees should be done, but feels uncomfortable doing. As a result, managers develop plans rather than visions. The result is compliance, not commitment. People say, "Yeah, that's your plan; you should have asked me for mine." Under compliance what you get from employees is their time (what they are getting paid for). They withhold their energy and simply produce. With employee commitment, however, you still get their time, but also their energy. They still produce, but also perform.

In general, it is essential to make a distinction between a plan and a vision. You can not say, "Here's my vision" and give people a plan. There is a very clear difference between them. Both are necessary, but the culture tends to reinforce going directly to the plan.

**A vision is where you are going;
a plan is how you get there.**

A good way to understand the difference between a vision and a plan is through an analogy from architecture. Imagine you wanted to build a house, and you went to an architect who interviewed you to find out what kind of house you wanted. When you went back a week later, he laid out very professionally drawn blueprints. What would you think? For one thing, you probably would be unable to read them. You would be frustrated. What if the architect said, "Well just change anything you want"? You could not do it because you would not have the expertise.

Rather than a blueprint, what you need is an artist's rendering, an illustration or model to precede the blueprint. With such a model you can actually see the house and mentally move around in it. Architects use an artist's rendering first because:

- It helps people understand what they are getting.
- It is easier for people to commit to a project when they can see the end result.

- The client can participate in the design process, make changes, and suggestions.
- It allows the architect and client to play with and form the idea.

The blueprint is the plan. The artist's rendering or model is the vision. This rendering will get people to commit to the building, not the blueprint. Just as organizations tend to jump to beginnings, they also tend to jump to blueprints—that is, to detailed plans and procedures.

This is not to say that the plan is not important. Ultimately you need the plan to do the actual work. However, if you begin by presenting plans and procedures, you push people toward the change. You will probably not have their commitment. In contrast, vision is like a magnet; it draws people toward it. Enabling the creation of a vision is a useful skill, particularly during a change situation, to align people on the purpose of the new direction. Visions create a "whole" in which you see yourself. Visions are pliable; you can participate in them and reshape them. Visions are also open; that is, blanks can be filled in. Finally, to be effective, visions are sensual.

CONCEPTUAL VERSUS SENSUAL VISIONS

To understand the difference in effect between a conceptual vision and a sensual one, consider the following two vacation "pitches" or visions.

> Let's go to Florida. We are going to have fun, relax, and have a good time. We can enjoy ourselves at the beach. We can swim. We can get a good tan, walk the beaches, and just take it easy. It will be great!

Compare the preceding with this:

> Imagine us, lying on the beach, the warm sand on our back, the sun on our faces, the smell of the salt air mingled with that of suntanning lotion, the palms swaying gracefully, the waves lapping up, the tepid breeze, the seagulls calling shrilly, children laughing, and a cool, refreshing dip in the crystal clear water.

Which one sells you more on going to Florida? The sensually oriented one. Which is more motivational? Again, the sensual. An effective vision, like a good story, draws people in with sights, sounds, feelings, even taste and smell. These elements create "whole" experiences rather than thoughts.

Keeping in mind the difference between a sensual and a conceptual vision, consider the phrase "to work as a high-performing team." What *is* a high-performing team? What does it look like, sound like, feel like? What would motivate you to want to be a member of such a team? Consider the following: "What I want to see around here is people talking to each other, feeling free to raise problems and share ideas without any fear of being told it won't work. I want to see open doors and people meeting in each other's offices, laughing, brainstorming, going over project plans, and feeling proud of our ideas and solutions." In this statement, the concept of a high-performing team takes on substance.

In view of the power of the sensual elements in a vision, the question arises: If it's so effective, why don't people do it more often? One answer is that our educational system teaches us to be conceptual. Concepts are an effective form of shorthand. With them you can express large classes of things in short statements. At times, however, you need to reverse this process and translate the concepts back into sensual raw material.

When seeing your doctor, for example, "I feel run down" is not good enough. You need to specify your symptoms: sore throat, headache, abdominal pain. When creating a vision for an organization, the same is true. "Good customer service" is not good enough. You need to specify what you want: Customers saying, "I appreciate your doing that for me," calling people back promptly, checking stock before making promises, listening carefully to complaints.

Martin Luther King's speech "I Have a Dream" is a classic example of vision elevated to the level of poetry. He did not just talk about freedom or rights or equality. Rather, he allowed his audience to *see* them. In the context of Biblical images of a view from "the mountain" and the "promised land," he talked about a black child and a white child playing together and people working as equals regardless of their skin color.

King's vision was just that—visual images strung together to create a sense of what the country could be.

Consider the vision of Steven Jobs, founder of Apple Computer. His vision of "computers in every home" evokes pictures of individuals and families working in their dens, living rooms, or kitchens—working, playing, and enjoying the convenience of a "personal" computer. His vision, of course, begs the questions: What will these computers look like? How will they work? How will we make them "friendly"? Such a vision motivates people to be creative—to come up with something that will fulfill the promise that the vision of a computer in every home conjures up.

Most managers are not a Martin Luther King or a Steven Jobs, but that does not mean they cannot motivate through visions. When Michael Blumenthal was president of Burroughs Corporation, he put his vision this way:

> We no longer have a philosophy of one product, one plant. We no longer look for volume for the sake of volume; we look for return on investment. We no longer look for accounting profits, we look for cash. We don't worry about getting shipments out by the end of the quarter if we are not sure they are 100 percent OK. We'll lose more business six months from now if we ship out lousy stuff. In the *new* Burroughs, we take pride and only ship out what works.

Burroughs' appeal for diversification and quality was a challenge to do business in a new way. Primarily, this vision went not for picture, but for attitudes. Granted, there are visual images such as "cash," "getting shipments out," and "lousy stuff." But his vision is primarily one which says: Take a new attitude toward your work, do what makes sense, and if something doesn't make sense any more, change it.

The implications of a vision like that are far reaching. For some, Blumenthal's vision might be a little disturbing, but in general it allowed people to apply their skills when and where they were needed. If a few rules were broken and a little temporary confusion resulted, it was certainly a small price to pay for the productivity, fulfillment, and fun that resulted.

In general, to create a vision is to create a whole—a whole into which people can project themselves. This "whole" might be a picture, an attitude, a feeling. Once people "get it," they begin to interpret, expand, and flesh it out in terms of their own jobs and lives.

The value of a vision is that it can serve as a unifying image or sense of what all the plans and procedures will look like when they are completed. A vision is future-focused.

Vision takes you from the past and commits you to the future.

Visioning, picturing what you want, can help avoid or minimize the problems associated with focusing on results. Consider, for example, the person who gives himself three months to find a job. If after the first month he is still searching, he may begin to perceive of himself as a failure. Rather, he should hold fast to his vision and learn from each unsuccessful application. Remember the story told about Thomas Edison: When asked how it felt to have failed 25,000 times to make a storage battery, he replied that he had not failed but, rather, that he had learned 25,000 ways NOT to make one.

COMMUNICATING A VISION

A vision is designed to be shared. Consider how Rick communicates his vision with his employees at Averco:

> RICK: We've been through a lot in the last six weeks. But I think we came through in one piece. I've talked to you each individually, and I think everyone's moving in the same direction in terms of accepting the change. Am I right?

(Everyone voices general agreement.)

> RICK: I called this meeting because I wanted to give you some sense of how I see this place working. I mean us. But first I'd like to give you a short history. Twenty years ago this company

started and it grew fast, and it diversified.
Before long we were into a lot of areas that
didn't even exist when we first started. Level
One grew to Level Two, Level Two to Level
Three, and then, eventually Level Four.
Things worked fine for a long time. But recently we've lost some of the market share,
specifically Level One offerings which used
to be, to borrow Paul's phrase, our bread and
butter. But, probably for sentimental reasons, we hung onto Level One for too long
because this is where we started—this was
the foundation of our company. And we ignored Level Four which is where the future
lies. So in reorganization we decided to
phase out Level One and push Level Four.
That's it. It's that simple.

(Rick pauses briefly, then continues.)

Now—the future. In the future this is what I
would like to see. The other day I was walking through your area, Paul, and I saw Jill
talking on the phone. She was talking to Al in
your department, Warren, and she was trying
to understand how your area worked, and she
was trying to communicate to him how her
area worked. There's nothing really earth-
shattering about that. It's just the attitude,
the way she went about it, the tremendous
energy and commitment she had. She was
earnestly trying to communicate. No false
pretense, she was genuinely interested. Think
about it. What's the likelihood of that happening in this group a month ago? Enough
said. That's what I would like to have happen
around here. People feeling free to cross the
lines, to go outside their area, to go outside
their turf and get to the other areas. You
might think of it this way. Picture a helicopter. The lower the helicopter flies, the
smaller the area of ground the people in it can
see. We've all been flying low lately—in
more ways than one.

WARREN: Yeah. We've been barely clearing the trees.

RICK: Exactly, Warren. We see small areas that don't
          overlap, and we communicate our perception
          of Averco from these positions. And since
          they don't overlap, it's difficult to appreciate
          someone else's point of view. We find our-
          selves arguing from *our* point of view. Now
          I'd like us all to fly higher so that our view is
          broader. Then we can communicate from a
          sense of the whole rather than from a limited
          perspective. And I think that's just exactly
          what Jill was doing.

PAUL: You know, Jill sets an example around here
          for all of us. Looking at her, we can all see
          how we *ought* to work together.

WARREN: It's not just Jill. I find it really helpful to see
          that kind of communication. But are you say-
          ing, Rick, that we should all begin to float a
          little?

RICK: Yes, I am. And we might look to Dennis in
          that regard.

DENNIS: Right. I guess I can serve as an example. I'm
          probably a professional floater.

JUDY: How do we do that?

RICK: Well, that's what we've got to figure out. For
          now I can only talk about it in examples
          and analogies like Jill and the helicopter. But
          the *idea* is valid—and essential. That's why
          I came to you. I don't have the master plan.
          We're going to have to work that out to-
          gether.

Rick began his presentation by giving some background
information ("grew fast and diversified"; "phased out Level
One and phased in Level Four"; "it's that simple"). Then he
explained that market share had slipped and that the company needed to recoup. After this brief history he changed
the tone to communicate the future. He wanted to give more
than just information; he wanted to give them a sense of how
he pictured the future. So he shifted gears. He went from a

conceptual kind of explanation to a very different approach as he started talking about his vision. He described Jill's activities, in a sound picture. Recognize that they all know who Jill is, where she sits, what she looks and sounds like. This simple example of Jill had the basic ingredients of sight, sound, and the feeling of commitment embodied by Jill. Rick used the example of Jill as an example of the spirit he wanted to see in the work unit.

Finally, shifting gears again, Rick introduced the helicopter analogy. This analogy was a means to talk about the outcome of a spirit like that of Jill. With both of these aspects of his vision on the table, Rick stopped and waited for a reaction.

Paul accepted the vision as the ideal to strive for. Warren immediately started to work out the implications for himself. And Judy asked the basic question, "How?" Even though their responses were varied, they did have one thing in common: involvement.

All of Rick's staff were beginning to explore the implications of Rick's sense of what they would need to do in the future. Rick presented a vision, not a plan. It had both conceptual and sensual elements. It was able to involve his teams without locking them into any specific course of action. It demanded their flying higher to get a greater sense of the whole.

STRATEGIES FOR NEW BEGINNINGS

Many activities make up the beginnings stage of a change. The items presented earlier, which included such activities as budgeting, staffing, establishing controls, and setting deadlines, are only a partial list. These are basically technical activities. A book could be written on each one, which is why this chapter chooses not to cover them. The focus here has been on some of the key interpersonal and context-setting skills so essential to successful beginnings. These are the skills that organizations tend to lose touch with when entering the normative period of their growth. These are nothing less than survival skills when an organization begins to grow out of that normative stage. The basic strategies that make up this survival kit are summarized in the following pages.

Encourage Symbols and Ceremonies

During change, symbols and ceremonies appear sponta-
neously. These can either support the change or oppose it. In
either case, they reflect the climate of the organization at
given times. Rumors and rumblings might begin to manifest
themselves as negative and sarcastic symbols and ceremonies.
If so, the organization needs to look at what it is doing.

In one company, for example, a reorganization resulted in
widespread dissatisfaction and attrition. The employees were
getting out, and as each one gave notice, he or she received a
number (#23, #24, etc.) which that person wore as a symbolic
badge of having beat the company. It got to the point where
there were actual ceremonies associated with assigning these
numbers and, as a result, the level of dissatisfaction and employee desire to leave only increased.

Because symbols and ceremonies are potentially so effective, organizations often strive to create them to help move a
change along. This impulse is a good one, but also one which
can work against the organization if it is not careful. Commonly, organizations use symbolic slogans such as "Quality
and Teamwork" or "We try harder." Such slogans are initially
just rhetoric. To make them function positively, the organization must follow up with action and symbolic behavior
from the leadership. Without this follow up, the slogan remains just a phrase and may even be turned against the
organization.

In one company, for example, the new slogan was "Everyone counts." But nothing changed, and a few weeks later, in a
hallway that had an "electronic eye" to monitor the people
traffic in that end of the building, someone placed a sign
reading "Everyone counts" next to the electronic monitor.

Organizations can also be responsive to the groundswell of
symbols and ceremonies that are already taking form. As
mentioned, the pink slip award was just such a spontaneous
symbol—a little offbeat perhaps, but one that expressed at a
gut level what was a very positive attitude. The organization
could have ignored this symbol, preferring its own "sanitized"
and management-generated slogan, but it chose to honor this
development and support it.

In summary, organizationally generated symbols and ceremonies must be backed up with actions. Also, the organization must realize that when it creates a symbol or ceremony, it ceases to "own" it. Once it is let into the organization, it takes on a life of its own. Any organizational attempt to leash it and make it mean only certain things may result in its turning sour. At Averco, for example, Averco Day was intended as a "Beginnings" ceremony. It turned out to be an "Endings/Transitions" ceremony. Recognizing that fact, the organization allowed it to take on its own meaning and by so doing, not only increased the ceremony's positive influence, but also demonstrated positive symbolic behavior by not trying to control the ceremony's development.

Keep Values Constant

In addition to symbols and ceremonies, the values honored by an organization are extremely important, particularly in times of change. The one constant in change is the organization's value system. This can be the "rock" which people in a change situation know will still be there for them. This value system may be associated with quality, full employment, openness, risk-taking, and the like. Whatever the value, it is important that the organization keep it both constant and visible.

One obstacle to keeping a value system both constant and visible can be understood in terms of one pair of words used on the Change Response Scale: form/purpose. The value system of a company is the "purpose." The old organization (pre-change) is the form. When the form changes, people often think that the purpose has changed as well. Usually this is not the case, but the perception exists, nevertheless. Therefore, when an organization experiences change (a new form), the organization's leadership may take for granted that employees realize that the value system (the purpose) is still intact. Meanwhile, within the organization, people equate the new change of form with a corresponding change of purpose and find evidence to support this perception.

The leadership of an organization must be sensitive to this potential misperception and take steps, via statements and behavior, to create and maintain the existing value system.

Recognize the People Symbolizing the New Beginning

In times of beginnings, it is important to acknowledge those people who best represent the new beginning. The organization needs to recognize the small core of people who are moving to new beginnings, and support and reward them. These people may be managers or they may be like the person who started the pink slip tradition. In any case, it is important to acknowledge those who are committed to the change and moving toward new beginnings.

Establish a System of High Communication

In new beginnings, it is essential to create an open-door philosophy that allows, indeed, encourages people to talk. Much information will be coming down, but for beginnings to succeed, information must also flow upward. The organization must structure itself to promote open communication at all levels, horizontally and vertically.

In one company, for example, when a new CEO was hired, the first thing he enacted was a chance for the entire organization to talk to upper management, himself included, on a weekly basis.

Or recall Cray's emphasis on verbal communication with its watchword, "Call, don't write."

Establish High-Performance Teams

This strategy could (and does) constitute the topic of an entirely different book. Nonetheless, the concept of teambuilding is critical during new beginnings. As the change progresses, one-on-one skills become much less important than group/ team-building skills. People need to feel a part of the whole. They need to be led-rather than "managed," and they need to know that they make a difference.

Be Future-Focused through Vision

An effective vision:

- Provides an enduring focus, where excellence is expected and energies are directed.

- Unites and inspires people to extra effort.
- Focuses energy on outcome, the whole rather than segments.
- Satisfies the need of the new, educated worker to be involved in making a difference.

Employees today want challenging, meaningful work and often place this ahead of rewards such as pay or status. People want to believe in something that can tap hidden personal resources—something that permits performance beyond normal commitment and energy. Vision helps them see the potential.

What seems to distinguish the truly successful business leaders is their clear, simple, and compelling sense of where they want their business or department to go and what they want to represent. Their power is drawn from conscious intention and vision, not blind intuition or orders from above.

The Law of the Higher Helicopter

Rick's analogy of the higher helicopter serves as good advice, not only for Averco, but for any company going through change. Phase II, for all its benefits such as comfort, profitability, and predictability, also fosters the tendency to fly low and keep your eyes on your turf. Functionalism promotes the idea that specific areas should not overlap. Leave the overview to upper management. That is *their* job. When they see that alterations need to be made, they will tell you. Then, and only then, will it be *your* job.

Such a point of view is appropriate in a period of normalcy, but when change occurs, these principles do not apply any longer. What is needed at these times is a rebirth of basic values associated with Phase I, namely, high commitment, the sense of employees being stakeholders in the organization's direction, empowerment of employees to initiate action, and the need for employees to have a sense of the whole.

Once individuals have worked through the particulars of their endings and have begun their journey of transition, the need for group interaction and group strategies becomes key. When employees reach this point in the change process, the organization nears critical mass: a smaller, but denser super-heated entity on the verge of experiencing a sudden surge of energy. Nothing can stop this surge. The key is to harness it—to help it move in the right direction.

10

REDUCING THE HALF-LIFE OF RECOVERY

Compared with what we ought to be,
we are only half awake.
William James

Never underestimate the value of a
change strategy. It can help you get
through the thing a whole lot quicker
than if you just let it happen to you.
Person experiencing two major
changes in five years

The *half-life* of a radioactive substance is the length of time it takes for half the substance to change from a radioactive unstable state to a nonradioactive stable state. If you have a pound of a substance with a half-life of ten years today, in ten years you will have a half pound, in another ten years a quarter of a pound, then an eighth, a sixteenth, and so on.

This information is useful when dealing with a real problem—for example, the disposal of radioactive waste. Simply stated, a substance with a half-life of 10,000 years is going to be a problem much longer than one with a half-life of two years. The substance with the two-year half-life will be pretty much gone in a decade; the substance with the 10,000 year half-life will remain at virtual full strength for thousands of years.

In response to a change, people have what can be called a half-life of recovery. If somebody changes your schedule, causing you inconvenience, you may initially be angry. After a few minutes, you will probably cool down so you are only "half" as angry. In ten minutes, you are probably over it and moving on to accept and deal with the situation. If you experience the death of a family member, that "half-life" is much longer. It might be a year before the loss is only "half" as painful and several years before you are "over it." But even ten years later, there will be pangs and twinges of the original pain.

HOW LONG IS YOUR HALF-LIFE OF RECOVERY?

The answer to that question depends on two factors: One, the nature of the change itself and two, how you deal with it. In most cases, the less intense the change, the shorter the half-life. But how you personally deal with the change can vary widely.

One man experienced two rather significant career changes in the period of five years. Both were painful, but necessary.

For the first one, the half-life was about a year; for the second, about two months.

Why the difference? With the first one, the man complained and stewed, played "Poor Me," and generally chose to keep the pain level high. With the second, he took the pain in large doses, tried to see his way through to the opportunities, and had pretty much moved through the process in about four months. Reflecting on the experience, he commented, "At first I thought the reason I handled the second change so much better was because I had learned my lesson in the first situation. But it was more than that. In the second situation, I thought things through, sought help, and got it. Never underestimate the value of a change strategy. It can help you get through the thing quicker than if you just let it happen to you."

If you think about the changes you have experienced in your life, you will probably discover that you also experienced half-lives of varying lengths.

When change occurs, people commonly go quickly from low pain to high pain. Then gradually (or not so gradually) the pain starts to decrease until eventually an hour, a day, a year, or five years later the pain level is low enough to allow them to can get on with their lives or jobs. The length of that slope from high to low pain depends on the half-life of that change.

Some people come down very quickly—but that is generally not the case. Some people choose to extend the high pain for a long time and may never come down. Dickens' character Miss Haversham in *Great Expectations*, in response to being jilted on her wedding day, chose to live the rest of her life in one room, with the moldering wedding cake, brooding over her fate. Thus the half-life of *her* change was longer than her natural life and she died in her own pain.

Like Miss Haversham, many of us choose to sustain our pain and drag it with us, like excess baggage, into the next episode of our life—where it becomes a burden to our growth.

In other cases, we are told by well-meaning people not to cry over spilt milk or to put the matter behind us and "get on with it." Unfortunately, this does not help much either because humans need at least *some* time to work through their losses—a subject which has been written about extensively.

In other words, you cannot choose *not* to have a half-life of

recovery, but you can have a say in how long it will last—
both for yourself and for those with whom you work.

The purpose of this book has been to focus on the personal
and organizational aspects of change—specifically, to recognize that different people and organizations will have different reactions to change and, therefore, different half-lives of
recovery. The intent is not to "solve" problems, nor even to
reduce the original pain. Rather, the intent is to help shorten
the half-life by providing insights and skills designed to allow
people and organizations to move more easily through the
change process.

RECOVERY AND THE "PAIN CHART" REVISITED

One way to visualize differences in half-lives—that is, differences in recovery rates—is by reviewing the "Pain Chart." As
explained in Chapter 3, when change occurs, people often
jump from low pain levels to high pain levels and then go
through a series of ups and downs, gradually returning to a
relatively low pain level, as shown in Figure 1.

Previously you saw how this chart reflected the difference
between Harry's change which was handled poorly in contrast to Steve's which was handled well. The same kind of
differences can occur at the organizational level.

In one company undergoing change, the normal period of
recovery for departments was about nine months. That is,
from the initial reorganization and the resultant drop in productivity and morale to the point at which acceptable levels

FIGURE 1

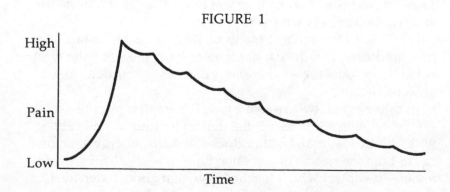

FIGURE 2

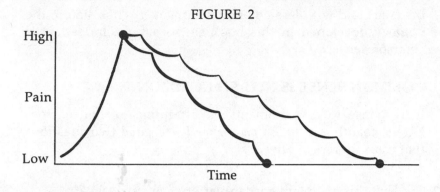

of productivity and morale were restored was about nine months. Two departments, however, had returned to those acceptable levels in about five to six months. The difference can be expressed as shown in Figure 2.

Why were these two departments able to recover more quickly? After all, they were, at the outset of the change, no different than the other people or departments in the company. As it turned out, the reason for the difference was that both departments developed and worked out a plan to address the endings of the individual employees and develop transitions strategies toward a clear vision of what the new beginning would be.

In short, the people managed themselves and managed their department in such a way as to reduce the half-life of the change and speed their own recovery.

When change occurs, a high or relatively high pain level is a given. Also, over time, this pain gradually diminishes and people and organizations move back to a sense of normalcy. The rate of this recovery, however, is *not* a given. It will vary, depending on the way it is handled, both personally and organizationally. This is not to say that you can skip the period of recovery altogether and suddenly drop from high to low pain. Such a claim would be unrealistic. But it *is* possible to shorten that recovery period.

By addressing the endings of individuals in an organization and developing a plan to move through transitions to beginnings, you can reduce the half-life of your recovery and move through the change process more quickly, with less people breakage and with less emotional carryover. Thus stated, the strategy developed in this book seems simple. Indeed, it is common sense.

COMMON SENSE IS NOT SO COMMON

In response to his comments on attaining excellence, Tom Peters, coauthor of *In Search of Excellence*, cited two questions that came up repeatedly:

1. Isn't this just plain garden-variety common sense?
2. And if so, why haven't we been practicing it?

Peters answers:

1. Yes.
2. I don't know.

In his mind, attaining excellence *is* just a matter of common sense. Even though he did not know for sure why people do not just *do* it, he offered a theory. "Perhaps the answer is," he says, "because it isn't magical enough. It isn't sophisticated and complicated."

There is a great deal of truth in Peters' statement. A craving for sophistication and uniqueness often clouds people's ability to recognize the value of that which is simple. Common sense often seems too mundane to be valuable. Recall the simple/complex versus easy/difficult learning model discussed earlier. The "N" progression from complex to simple and then difficult to easy is obvious in the case of physical activity like skiing, golf, or running marathons. Nobody can read a book on one of those subjects and claim mastery of it. A book may help in some ways, but the student still has to get snow in his mouth, land in sand traps, and endure shin splints before the activity even approaches easy.

In the area of management and interpersonal skills, however, people tend to forget that there is a right-hand side to the learning model. They fall back on the comfort of their academic inclinations and prefer to read about, discuss, theorize, attend lectures, take classes, anything to avoid *doing*. They ask, "Isn't this just common sense?" Or complain, "This isn't very sophisticated, is it?"

Peters was correct. People want things to be "sophisticated"—that is, they prefer to challenge their intellect rather than subject themselves to the discomfort of an apprenticeship of action.

Therefore, the challenge of *Aftershock* is for you to take the concepts and models presented and TRY THEM OUT.

APPENDIX A

A LIST OF TECHNICAL, POLITICAL, AND CULTURAL SYSTEM RESISTANCES*

Technical System Resistances include:

Habit and inertia. Habit and inertia cause task-related resistance to change. Individuals who have always done things one way may not be politically or culturally resistant to change, but may have trouble, for technical reasons, changing behavior patterns. Example: some office workers may have difficulty shifting from electric typewriters to word processors.

Fear of the unknown or loss of organizational predictability. Not knowing or having difficulty predicting the future creates anxiety and hence resistance in many individuals. Example: the introduction of automated office equipment has often been accompanied by such resistance.

Sunk costs. Organizations, even when realizing that there are potential payoffs from a change, are often unable to enact a change because of the sunk costs of the organizations' resources in the old way of doing things.

Political System Resistances include:

Powerful coalitions. A common threat is found in the conflict between the old guard and the new guard. One interpretation of the exit of Archie McGill, former president of the newly formed

---

* Source: Noel M. Tichy, *Managing Strategic Change: Technical, Political, and Cultural Dynamics*. New York: John Wiley & Sons, 1983.

AT&T American Bell, is that the backlash of the old-guard coalition exacted its price on the leader of the new-guard coalition.
Resource limitations. In the days when the economic pie was steadily expanding and resources were much less limited, change was easier to enact as every part could gain—such was the nature of labor management agreements in the auto industry for decades. Now that the pie is shrinking, decisions need to be made as to who shares a smaller set of resources. These zero-sum decisions are much more politically difficult. As more and more U.S. companies deal with productivity, downsizing, and divestiture, political resistance will be triggered.

Indictment quality of change. Perhaps the most significant resistance to change comes from leaders having to indict their own past decisions and behaviors to bring about a change. Example: Roger Smith, chairman and CEO of GM, must implicitly indict his own past behavior as a member of senior management when he suggests changes in GM's operations. Psychologically, it is very difficult for people to change when they were party to creating the problems they are trying to change. It is much easier for a leader from the outside, such as Lee Iacocca, who does not have to indict himself every time he says something is wrong with the organization.

Cultural System Resistances include:

Selective perception (cultural filters). An organization's culture may highlight certain elements of the organization, making it difficult for members to conceive of other ways of doing things. An organization's culture channels that which people perceive as possible; thus, innovation may come from outsiders or deviants who are not as channeled in their perceptions.

Security based on the past. Transition requires people to give up the old ways of doing things. There is security in the past, and one of the problems is getting people to overcome the tendency to want to return to the "good old days." Example: today, there are still significant members of the white-collar workforce at GM who are waiting for the "good old days" to return.

Lack of climate for change. Organizations often vary in their conduciveness to change. Cultures that require a great deal of conformity often lack much receptivity to change. Example: GM with its years of internally developed managers must overcome a limited climate for change.

REFERENCES

Ainsworth-Land, George. *Grow or Die.* New York: John Wiley & Sons, 1986.

Bennis, Warren and Nanus, Burt. *Leaders: The Strategies for Taking Charge.* New York: Harper & Row, 1985.

Bridges, W. *Transitions: Making Sense of Life's Changes.* Reading, MA: Addison-Wesley, 1980.

Deal, Terrence E. and Kennedy, Allen A. *Corporate Cultures.* Reading, MA: Addison-Wesley, 1982.

Enright, John. "Change and Resilience." *The Leader Manager,* Eden Prairie, MN: Wilson Learning Corporation, 1984, pp. 59–73.

Gerber, Beverly. "The Forgotten Factor in Merger Mania," *Training,* February 1987, pp. 20–37.

Hage, Dave. "Tale of Plant-Closing May End with Different Twist," *Minneapolis Star and Tribune,* November 25, 1986, p. 7b.

Kanter, Rosabeth Moss. *The Changemasters.* New York: Simon and Schuster, 1983.

Lashbrook, Velma J. "Victims or Agents of Change: The Choice is Ours." Eden Prairie, MN: Wilson Learning Corporation, 1985.

Peters, Thomas J. and Waterman, Robert H. Jr. *In Search of Excellence.* New York: Harper & Row, 1982.

Tichy, Noel M. *Managing Strategic Change: Technical, Political, and Cultural Dynamics.* New York: John Wiley & Sons, 1983.

Tichy, Noel M. and Ulrich, David O. "SMR Forum: The Leadership Challenge—A Call for the Transformational Leader." *Sloan Management Review,* Fall 1984, pp. 59–68.

Tofler, Alvin. *Future Shock.* New York: Bantam Books, 1970.

Willins, Harold. *The Trim Tab Factor.* New York: William Morrow and Company, Inc., 1984.

INDEX